Louis Albert Banks

The Saloon-Keeper's Ledger

A Series of Temperance Revival Discourses

Louis Albert Banks

The Saloon-Keeper's Ledger
A Series of Temperance Revival Discourses

ISBN/EAN: 9783337817442

Printed in Europe, USA, Canada, Australia, Japan

Cover: Foto ©Thomas Meinert / pixelio.de

More available books at **www.hansebooks.com**

THE
SALOON-KEEPER'S LEDGER

A Series of Temperance Revival Discourses

BY

REV. LOUIS ALBERT BANKS, D.D.

AUTHOR OF "THE PEOPLE'S CHRIST," "WHITE SLAVES," "THE REVIVAL QUIVER," "COMMON FOLKS' RELIGION," "THE HONEY-COMBS OF LIFE," "HEAVENLY TRADE-WINDS," "CHRIST AND HIS FRIENDS," ETC.

WITH INTRODUCTION BY
THE REV. THEODORE L. CUYLER, D.D.

PRINTED IN THE UNITED STATES

NEW YORK
FUNK & WAGNALLS COMPANY
LONDON AND TORONTO
1895

CONTENTS.

	PAGE
INTRODUCTION	7

ITEM NUMBER ONE.
   The Saloon Debtor to Disease 11

ITEM NUMBER TWO.
   The Saloon Debtor to Private and Social Immorality, 32

ITEM NUMBER THREE.
   The Saloon Debtor to Ruined Homes 49

ITEM NUMBER FOUR.
   The Saloon Debtor to Pauperized Labor 66

ITEM NUMBER FIVE.
   The Saloon Debtor to Lawlessness and Crime . . 81

ITEM NUMBER SIX.
   The Saloon Debtor to Political Corruption 94

HOW TO SETTLE THE SALOON ACCOUNT 112

INTRODUCTION.

BY REV. THEODORE L. CUYLER, D.D.

MY eloquent friend and neighbor, Dr. Louis Albert Banks, has been doing what every pastor may wisely imitate. He has been giving his own people, and the large numbers outside of his own membership who resort to the Hanson Place M. E. Church, a series of most instructive discourses on the vital question of Temperance.

For a whole week the spacious church edifice was thronged on every evening; and several neighboring ministers were called in to preside at these large assemblages, and to offer their own brief contribution of practical truth.

The crying need of the hour is a *fresh education* of the public mind and conscience in regard to the curse of strong drink. The reason why laws prohibiting the sale of intoxicants are not passed — or if passed are left in some places to become a dead letter — is that the majority of the people in such places believe in buying and in drinking intoxicants. The public sentiment in those localities has no backbone of Total Abstinence in it.

There must be a new education of the American people in regard to the drink-evil. It must be carried on in the homes, in the Sunday-school, in the public schools, and from the pulpits. General Neal Dow wrought for many years in such an educational campaign before Maine enacted her first prohibitory law.

Social drinking customs are sadly on the increase. The decanters are stealing back into families from whom we expect better things. Too many pulpits are either silent, or speak "with bated breath." The church of Jesus Christ must come up to its full measure of duty if the drinking customs are to be changed and the drink traffic to be suppressed.

Temperance ballots are not self-made; they are the result of education and the toning-up of the public conscience.

Dr. Banks has set a splendid example; and this volume, containing his recent lectures, is most heartily recommended, and deserves a broadcast circulation.

BROOKLYN, May 11, 1895.

TO MY FRIENDS

Charles C. and Frances A. Beveridge

THE SWEET SINGERS OF THE PROHIBITION
EVANGEL,

WHOSE CHARMING SONGS DID SO MUCH TO MAKE THE
DISCOURSES RECORDED HEREIN EFFEC-
TIVE WHEN DELIVERED,

This Volume

IS AFFECTIONATELY DEDICATED BY

THE AUTHOR.

THE SALOON-KEEPER'S LEDGER.

ITEM NUMBER ONE.

THE SALOON DEBTOR TO DISEASE.

OUR theme in this series of evening conferences is to be "The Saloon-keeper's Ledger." You all understand what a ledger is. It is a book of results. Its balance sheets are the accumulated harvest of day-book and journal. The people of Brooklyn have had business with the saloon for a good many years. The day-books of every-day occurrences have passed into the journal of the years, and these have crystallized into a ledger of public knowledge. The liquor saloon, like any other business, must stand or fall by its ledger.

We come this evening to discuss the first item in the account. It is my purpose to deliberately charge and to prove that the saloon as an institution is the source of a large part of the disease in the community. Not only so, but I stand ready to show by the best scientific and medical authority on earth that the claim made by the organs of the liquor traffic, that intoxicating drinks are to be numbered among the necessities of life as food materials, is a delusion and a fraud.

Every kind of intoxicant sold by the liquor saloons and sought after by the debauched appetite is drunk for the sake of the alcohol it contains. Leave alcohol out of lager beer, and a man would as soon suck a faucet from an offal wagon as touch the nasty stuff. It is for the alcohol that is in it that the drinker is willing to swallow the slop. I have heard of a boy who was smoking his first cigar, and, becoming very pale and sick in countenance, said to his playmate as he threw it away, "There's something in that cigar that makes me sick." "I know what it is," said the other boy; "it's ter-backer." Alcohol is at once the basis and the devil of all intoxicating drink. Dr. Willard Parker, voicing the sentiment of medical science, pronounces alcohol "an irritant poison, having no place in a healthy system." Horace Greeley, in an earnest temperance editorial in the *Tribune* many years ago, urged young men to avoid the tempter in whatever form he might appear, "whether as punch or bitters, as sherry or madeira, as hock or claret, as heidsieck or champagne." Other members of the editorial corps who were not total abstainers greeted Mr. Greeley on his entrance to the office that morning with uproarious laughter, telling him that heidsieck was not a different wine from champagne, but only a particular brand. As the laugh went around the room, Mr. Greeley said, "Well, boys, I guess I'm the only man in this office that could have made that mistake. It don't matter what you call him — champagne, or heidsieck, or absinthe — he is the same old devil." There is no fact more absolutely established by science or history than that all alcoholic beverages have in them the "same old devil" — the sleepless enemy of health.

There is no greater delusion than the notion that the popular saloon drinks are aids to physical development, and of food value. Dr. A. E.

T. Longhurst, in the *Westminster Review*, says: "The stimulating action which alcohol appears to exert on the physical functions is only a paralytic action. Again, there is a strong belief that alcohol gives new strength and energy after fatigue has set in : the sensation of fatigue is one of the safety-valves of our machine. To stifle the feeling of fatigue in order to be able to work on, is like forcibly closing the safety-valve, so that the boiler may be over-heated, and explosion result. The belief that alcohol gives strength to the weary is particularly dangerous to the class of people whose income is already insufficient to procure subsistence, and who are misled by this prejudice into spending a large part of their earnings on alcoholic drinks, instead of purchasing good and palatable food, which alone can give them strength for their hard work. It is commonly thought that alcoholic drinks aid digestion ; but in reality the contrary would appear to be the case, for it has been proved that a meal without alcohol is more quickly followed by hunger than when it is taken." A great German chemist, after many years of thorough experiment, says : " I have proved with mathematical accuracy that the amount of nourishment you may take up on the point of a table-knife inserted into a sack of flour contains absolutely more nourishment for the physical organism than the nourishment contained in eight quarts of the best Bavarian beer; and if a person is able to drink two gallons of beer each day in the year, he would get about the same amount of nutrition from the beer in twelve months that he would by consuming a five-pound loaf of bread, or three pounds of lean meat."

If you have a mathematical head you can easily compute, according to this chemist — who is also a German — that in attempting to get food out of beer a man has to strain one hundred and twenty gallons of swill through his disgusted stomach in order to catch a loaf of bread.

Not only is the beer which is in common use in Brooklyn of no value for food, but it is a great and prolific source of disease. The *Toledo Blade* some years ago made one of the most searching investigations into the beer question ever made in this country or any other. It presented the opinions of the leading physicians of the whole world in regard to the effect of beer on the physical health. Without exception, these medical men condemned its use, and declared that it was especially fruitful in producing diseases of the liver and kidneys, and in all cases lowered the vital forces to such a point that disease had little to do to sweep its beer-drinking victims out of the world. One physician said that in his own practice and observation forty-nine out of fifty cases of Bright's disease of the kidneys were cases of beer-drinkers. The evidence that was gathered at that time was summed up in this editorial utterance: "The indictment they of one accord present against beer-drinking is simply terrible. It is a curse for which there is no mitigation. The fearful devil-fish, crushing a fisherman in its long, winding arms, and sucking his life-blood from his mangled body and limbs, is not so frightful an assailant as this deadly but insidious enemy, which fastens itself upon its victim, and daily becomes more and more the wretched man's master, clogging up his liver, rotting his kidneys, decaying his heart and arteries, stupefying and starving his brain, choking his lungs and bronchia, loading his body down with dropsical fluids and unwholesome fat, fastening upon him rheumatism, erysipelas, and all manner of painful and disgusting diseases, and finally dragging him down to the grave at a time when other men are in their prime of mental and bodily vigor. Every one of them bears testimony to the fact that no man can drink beer safely; that it is an injury to any one who uses it in any quantity."

I press this question of beer home upon your attention, because I am satisfied that there is more danger at this point than at any other for young men — and young women too. Since I became pastor of this church a respectable young married woman told me, as an excuse for not giving me her church letter, that she had become so accustomed to drinking beer that she did not feel that she could get along without it. I am satisfied that this insidious enemy is making fresh inroads into respectable homes, and needs to be met by the repeated statement of the truth, and the setting forth of the facts with the greatest possible clearness.

Another argument on this beer question that ought to be conclusive to any intelligent man or woman is this: Milwaukee, Wisconsin, is the seat of one of the heaviest beer plants of this country. All over the West you see Milwaukee beer advertised as being especially good for the health, the claim being made that it is a health-giving liquid, and that its use conduces to longevity. Now, the Northwestern Life Insurance Company of Milwaukee was established in that city nearly, perhaps quite, forty years ago; it, too, is advertised all over the land as one of the great life insurance companies of the world, and as being especially wide-awake and shrewd in the management of its business. The greater number, if not all, of its directors are wealthy and responsible men of the city of Milwaukee and the State of Wisconsin. Having lived neighbors to this lager beer business, they have watched its growth and its influence on the consumers. Surely it is interesting to know what conclusion these sensible, hard-headed directors of a life insurance company have reached in regard to the beer question. It is this: Knowing all about the healthfulness of lager beer, they have come to the conclusion that for their own sake, for the protection of their own business, they can no longer grant a life insurance policy to a lager-beer brewer, no matter if he be a total abstainer at the time of application. They find that for such men the words of the poet are true:—

> "The grave doth gape
> For thee thrice wider than for other men."

Brewers are liable to exceptional temptations, to which many of them succumb. So this hard-headed life insurance company will not grant a policy to a lager-beer brewer, to his clerk, to his book-keeper, or the man who hauls his kegs, or to any man employed about the brewery. Why? These business-men say: "Because our statistics — which we have accumulated not as the result of fanaticism, or from any sentimental attempt to reform mankind; not because we pity the widows and orphans, but because we pity our own treasury — show that our business has been injured by the shortened lives of these men who drink lager beer." What better testimony do you want than that?

Solomon's question, "Who hath redness of eyes?" is answered now as of old upon every Brooklyn street where men tarry at the saloon. The dram-drinker's nose gets as red as his eyes, and frequently the rest of his face is as red as either. Dr. J. B. Johnson of Washington gives this reason for the redness of eyes and nose of the dram-drinker. He says: "The dram-drinker's heart beats about thirteen times oftener in a minute than the heart of one who does not drink alcohol. The arteries, in consequence of this increased heart action, carry the blood to the nose quicker than the veins carry it back. The blood, therefore, remains congested in the over-filled vessels, and the nose, and the face as well, become habitually red. So stagnant is this blood, that when the dram-drinker's nose meets a sudden current of cold air, it immediately turns purple, and so remains until warm air restores the red color. So the red nose is caused by congestion. Every organ of the body is in a similar state — a warning of an impending fate not to be avoided."

A man who was accustomed to indulge, entered a room of a hotel where a grave Quaker was sitting by the fire. Lifting a pair of green spectacles up on his forehead, and rubbing his inflamed eyes, the new-comer called for hot brandy and water. While he was waiting for it, he complained to the old Quaker that his eyes were getting weaker and weaker, and that the spectacles did not seem to do him any good. "I'll tell thee, friend," replied the Quaker, "what I think. It is that if thee were to wear the spectacles over thy mouth for a few months thy eyes would get well again."

But it is argued that in the great heat of summer we certainly need these drinks — some of them, at least — in a moderate degree. Well, let us put on the stand a world-famed and impartial observer — Henry M. Stanley, the African explorer. At a great meeting in New York City, after his return from the founding of the Congo State, and just before going back to Africa in search of Emin Pasha, Mr. Stanley, while addressing the Methodist Preachers' Meeting, made this reply to questions concerning the health of tropical climates : —

"You ask about the climate and healthfulness of the river valleys. How can you understand unless I specify certain points to illustrate? A man has been with me on the upper Congo two years and nine months. He has distinguished himself. I can recommend him to anybody for industry, fidelity, and attention to his duties. I wish to preserve him. He has slight dysenteric symptoms. I say to him: 'If I thought I could keep you from wine and liquor, I would send you to the coast, and send you home with good care; and if I had authority to bind you under an oath, so that you could not touch a glass of liquor, I should be quite sure that you would arrive at home, and after a residence there of from three to six months you would be prepared to return.' He said: 'But I promise you that I will not touch a drop of liquor.'—'I do not want to exercise any restraint over you, but my firm conviction is that if you do touch it you will never reach home. Good-by. Boys, carry him.'

"I give him a dozen hammock-bearers. He reaches the coast. The doctors attend him. He recovers from the slight dysenteric malady. They say that now he is in a fit condition to go home. That evening he swaps his coat to a native for a bottle of gin, and by midnight he is dead.

"Lieutenant Grant is a splendid, stalwart-looking man from Luxembourg. He has an ambition to distinguish himself. He does not like the post assigned him; so I give him other work, and fifty men to continue the road from Manyanga to Stanley Pool. He has with him one bottle of Burgundy. He will keep that for a gala day — the birthday of the king. He means to drink that to a large number of days to his Majesty. Some five miles on the road he meets a friend coming from Stanley Pool, and 'How do you do? I am delighted to see you.' The friend has just one bottle of brandy. They club together, and bring out, the one his bottle of Burgundy, and the other the brandy. Next morning the work must go on, of course. The trader bids him 'good-by,' and the officer must muster his working parties and proceed. But the effect of that night's dissipation is pretty soon seen. At nine o'clock the sun comes out strong. Before six o'clock that afternoon he is in his grave.

"There was a Scotch engineer who came out

recommended by the British East India Company. He was a genius. He knew the tricks of making the rudest structure comfortable and home-like. He takes charge of the steamer *Belgic* to go down to the mouth of the Congo. Three days afterward I ask the captain where his engineer is. He is dead. He was found sitting on a chair with a bottle of brandy in his hand — dead."

I think that will answer for heat.

With the usual inconsistency of a bad cause, it is argued that in a rigorous climate one needs the warmth of alcoholic stimulation. But this, again, is contrary both to science and observation. General Greely and Lieutenant Schwatka, the two most successful travelers of the English race who have made successful explorations in the frozen regions, unite in bearing testimony that the total abstainer, and not the moderate drinker, can best stand the rigor of a cold climate.

Every time of epidemic tells the same story over and over, that even moderate drinkers of intoxicants thereby destroy the power of their system to resist disease. During the epidemic of cholera in New York City in 1832, of two hundred and four cases in the Park Hospital, only six were temperate, and all of these recovered; while one hundred and twenty-two of the others died. In Great Britain in the same year five-sixths of all who perished were intemperate. In one or two villages every drunkard died, while not a single member of a temperance society lost his life. In Paisley, England, in 1848, there were three hundred and thirty-seven cases of cholera, and every case except one was a dram-drinker. The cases of cholera were one for every one hundred and eighty-one inhabitants; but among the temperate portion, there was only one case to each two thousand. Of three hundred and eighty-six persons connected with the total abstinence societies only one died; and he was a reformed drunkard who had been a member of the temperance society only three months, and had not outlived the effects of former intemperance. In New Orleans, during the last epidemic, the order of the Sons of Temperance appointed a committee to ascertain the number of deaths from cholera among their members. It was found that there were twelve hundred and forty-three members in the city and suburbs; and among these only three deaths had occurred, being only one-sixth the average death-rate. In New York City, in 1832, only two out of five thousand members of temperance societies died. A distinguished New York physician in commenting on the situation at the time said: "Had it not been for the sale and use of spirits there had not been cholera enough in the city to have caused the cessation of business for a single day." In the city of Washington the health authorities became so convinced of the dangers of the drinking habit in connection with cholera, that they caused the saloons to be closed three months. What a pity they couldn't have a cholera scare in Washington every time Congress meets!

The same testimony comes from every yellow-fever epidemic that sweeps over the South. Petroleum V. Nasby's humorous statement is verified over again every year in every saloon-cursed city in the land. Nasby makes Bascom, the keeper of the "wet grocery" at the Corners, say regretfully: "And then deth is another drorbak to my biznes. Ef a man cood only drink reglar, and live to be seventy, it wood be wuth while. But they don't do it. They are cut off by the crooel hand of deth jest when they begin to be yoosful to me. This one goes uv liver disease; t'other one uv kidney trouble; roomatism sets in and knocks one uv'm off his pins, and softenin' uv the brane kills another."

Now, then, this is the constant and never-ceasing tendency of the saloon. It undermines the health of the strongest laborer, unsettles the brain of the physician and the lawyer, as well as the man of business. In the language of an oft-quoted description: "What wreck is more shocking to behold than the wreck of a dissolute man?—the vigor of life exhausted, and yet the first steps of an honorable career not taken; in himself a lazar-house of disease; dead, but, by a heathenish custom of society, not buried. Rogues have had the initial letter of their title burned in the palms of their hands. Even for murder Cain was only branded in the forehead; but over the whole person of the debauchee or the inebriate the signature of infamy is written. How nature brands him with stigma and opprobrium! How she hangs labels all over him to justify her disgust and to admonish others to beware of his example! How she loosens all his joints, sends tremors along the muscles, and bends forward his frame, as if to bring him upon all fours, like kindred brutes, or to degrade him to the reptile's crawling! How she disfigures his countenance, as if intent upon obliterating all traces of her own image, that she may swear she never made him! How she pours rheum over his eyes, sends foul spirits to inhabit his breath, and shrieks as with a trumpet from every pore of his body, 'Behold the beast!'"

Now, you must all bear witness that I tell you the truth when I say that it is no accident, nothing uncommon, but only its ordinary, legitimate work, when the liquor saloon produces a result like that. Let the saloon stand or fall by its ledger.

John B. Finch once addressed a large audience at an agricultural fair in a Western State on the subject of prohibition. In the afternoon he was walking about the grounds, when a man came to him and said: —

"Your name is Finch; you are the man who talked temperance this forenoon?"

"Yes; or prohibition."

"Well, it all means the same thing."

Finch told him some people thought so.

"Now," said he, "I do not want to insult you; but I am a liquor dealer, and the managers of this fair did a dirty, mean thing in getting you here. This fair represents all the industries, and mine is a legitimate business. For them to get anybody here at a public fair to bring into disrepute one of the industries of the county is mean."

Mr. Finch replied, "It does look as though there was reason for your complaint. My friend, I believe you have been insulted, and if I were in your place I would go over to the president's office and kick up the biggest row they ever had on this ground. You say this is for all the industries of the county." (He took out of his pocket a premium list, and continued.) "Here is a premium for the nicest horses, the nicest cows, the best calves; for chickens, ducks, turkeys, and geese; for beets, turnips, squashes, and potatoes; for farm machinery; for all kinds of ladies' work; for cheese and butter. The managers of this fair seem to have offered a premium to encourage every industry but yours. If I were you I would raise a row."

The liquor man, considerably nonplussed, said, "What do you mean?"

Mr. Finch replied, "You do a legitimate business. You are manufacturing and turning your products out all the time. They ought to offer a premium on some of your finished jobs. They ought to put down twenty-five dollars for the best specimen of bummer made in a grog-shop in this county; fifteen dollars for the next; ten dollars for the next; and a red ribbon for the fourth. If you will go with me to the president, we will give him fits for not doing it."

But somehow that did not satisfy the liquor seller, but made him madder than ever. And yet that is the legitimate business of the liquor saloon — to prey upon the health and strength of the community, and leave it broken, diseased, and debauched. And I call upon you every one to witness that this is the usual, ordinary, and logical work of a liquor saloon; and that every time you by your influence, your negligence, or your vote, help to establish or continue a liquor saloon in the city of Brooklyn, you are helping to establish or continue a manufactory of disease, and a dangerous threat against the public health.

ITEM NUMBER TWO.

THE SALOON DEBTOR TO PRIVATE AND SOCIAL IMMORALITY.

THERE is a remarkable little book by Dr. Clokley of New Albany, Indiana, entitled "Dying at the Top," which, if I could, I would gladly put in the hands of every young man in America. The theme is drawn from a favorite apricot-tree that for many years stood in the author's dooryard, the very symbol of life and vigor. Its beautiful blossoms were always among the earliest heralds of the springtime, and the most delicious fruit soon followed the falling of the bloom. The tree was his pride and delight; but one day he saw that the very topmost branches had withered, and he said, "Ah, our apricot-tree is death-smitten; it is dying at the top." He carefully pruned off the top branches; but the next season still others were withered, and in a little while there was not enough life left in the tree to mature the few blossoms that it put forth. On a careful examination he found that worms were at work at the root of the tree. They had worked their way up under the bark; and, though the outside seemed firm and healthy, the tree was almost girdled by the unseen pests, and its death was inevitable.

From the dying of the tree-top came the study of the young human tree. If we accept as true Goethe's statement that "the destiny of any nation at any given time depends on the opinions of the young men who are under twenty-five years of age," then the facts massed by this student of young American manhood are full of the most serious peril. He finds by the most carefully scrutinized statistics that one-fourth of the entire male population of the country, or about seven and a half millions, are young men between eighteen and thirty years of age. Young men of these ages form one-sixth of the entire population of our thriving cities, and those between twenty-one and thirty-one are almost one-half of our voting population. What a momentous statement it is to make, that, in the immorality of this great class,

American society is "dying at the top." But after we have spent a few minutes looking at the facts, we are by no means ready to scout the statement.

You surely have noticed that nearly every specimen of the great army of tramps — numbering perhaps now nearly two hundred thousand men — who calls at your door is a young man. The universal testimony of railroad conductors and sheriffs, and all who have a special opportunity for observation, is that the overwhelming majority of these vagrants are but a little out of their boyhood, and nearly all of them under middle age. If I were speaking of crime as a whole, I could show you that sixty-seven out of one hundred of the entire criminal class of the country are young men.

But I have a far more delicate and difficult task before me to-night, and a task that somebody must perform. It is a dreadful comment on the so-called modesty of the Christian world that its magazines, newspapers, and pulpits have been almost wholly silent on the so-called social vices, except as now and again they are portrayed in sensational accounts of crime.

"Hush! hush!" the refined have cried at every public reference to them, till licentiousness has well nigh undermined our social fabric. Its prevalence is truly appalling. The better classes have been ignorant of it, because it is a malady that moves in silence, and preys on its victims in the night-time and in concealment. It has no plain advertisements in the newspapers; pastes up no flaming posters; glows with no electric lights; is surrounded by no bands of music. It is this secrecy that leaves so many parents and reformers in ignorance, and, when the thin veil is lifted, makes them incredulous of what is revealed. Certainly no other duty is more imperative in its demands upon the public teacher than to call serious attention to the raging and destroying sins of these great cities; the sin that lurks and corrupts unseen, and whose wide devastation is so much shielded by a false delicacy, or by circumstances which make men shrink as conscious that they lack skill, tact, and knowledge wisely to touch the most immedicable of evils. Listen to me, O young man, while I read the words of one of the wisest of observers that has ever lived.

Hear Solomon in the seventh chapter of Proverbs: "Say unto wisdom, Thou art my sister; and call understanding thy kinswoman: that they may keep thee from the strange woman, from the stranger that flattereth with her words. For at the window of my house I looked through my casement, and beheld among the simple ones, I discerned among the youths, a young man void of understanding, passing through the street near her corner; and he went the way to her house, in the twilight, in the evening, in the black and dark night: and, behold, there met him a woman with the attire of an harlot, and subtile of heart. . . . So she caught him, and kissed him, and with an impudent face said unto him, I have peace offerings with me; this day have I payed my vows. Therefore came I forth to meet thee, diligently to seek thy face, and I have found thee. I have decked my bed with coverings of tapestry, with carved works, with fine linen of Egypt. I have perfumed my bed with myrrh, aloes, and cinnamon. Come, let us take our fill of love until the morning: let us solace ourselves with loves. For the goodman is not at home, he is gone a long journey: he hath taken a bag of money with him, and will come home at the day appointed. With her much fair speech she caused him to yield, with the flattering of her lips she forced him. He goeth after her straightway, as an ox goeth to the slaughter, or as a fool to the correction of the stocks; till a dart strike through his liver; as a bird hasteth to the snare, and knoweth not that it is for his life. . . . Let not thine heart decline to her ways, go not astray in her paths. For she hath cast down many wounded: yea, many strong men have been slain by her. Her house is the way to hell, going down to the chambers of death."

If Solomon had lived in our time he would have seen that back of this poor lost woman, whose house is the way to hell, there is an innocent girlhood; and the coming into her young life of an impure and unholy influence, which has at first deceived and led her astray, and so made of her the social pariah that she is to-day. Dr. Flower, in the *Arena*, truly says: "Nowhere is the absolute brutality of society so painfully apparent as in the treatment of women who have stepped aside from the paths of virtue. Nowhere is the revolting moral obliquity of society so manifest as in the treatment of the fallen man who corrupts virginity. The girl to-day who falls under stress of circumstances which might well appal the strongest heart, is exiled and driven to the lowest depths. The betrayer of this same maiden, even though his crime be known, is welcomed into the homes of people who call themselves respectable, is permitted to marry a pure girl, and become the father of children cursed before they are born with the lecherous appetites of a morally depraved man. No better condition can be brought about without plain speaking; and though the subject is a painful and exceedingly unpleasant one, it is the duty of those who believe that an enduring civilization is possible only where steady morality prevails, to face this question with perfect frankness, no matter how much it may offend the lepers of conventional society or shock a sickly sentimentality."

The Chicago *Inter-Ocean*, commenting on the fact that out of thirty-two young men in New York City who were examined for a West Point cadetship, only nine were accepted as physically sound, says: "Such a note might well make the young men of our cities pause for a moment's thought. Beer, the cigarette, too much amusement, and the hidden vices, are making havoc with the physical manhood of all our towns and cities." A leading railroad man who had a large number of men under him, stated that so far as he was able to find out, every one of them was in the habit of visiting brothels. Another employer said, "I have twenty-five men under me, and only three of them refrain from intoxicating drinks." When asked how many of them refrained from sinning with women, he hesitated a moment, and then replied, "About as many."

These terrible facts mean not only the utter overthrow of young men, but of thousands of the fairest and truest young women. Throughout all the land hundreds of homes are being plundered of their most priceless jewels. That old legend of a monster, to satisfy whose voracious appetite a city had year by year to sacrifice a number of its virgins, who, amid the lamentation of their mothers and the grief of their kindred, were led away trembling to his bloody den, is no fable here in Brooklyn and New York. The monster is among us. Do you know what is the inevitable result of such a sowing? It can only by the very law of cause and effect produce a ruinous harvest.

If we do not want such a harvest, we must cease to sow that kind of seed. Tramps and scoundrels and criminals and ruined women are as certainly manufactured articles as Brussels carpets or locomotive engines. If we do not wish to produce them by our civilization, we have only to remove the causes of which they are the result. Junius Henri Brown states his belief in heredity thus: "The Rothschilds have been men possessed of rare genius for pecuniary planning, and for bearing the largest and most difficult enterprises to successful issues. They transmit the properties, material and mental, which they have inherited. Their blood flows in kindred channels generation after generation, and every drop of it dances to the jingle of coin. From foundation to turret they are built up and bulwarked with cash. In due process of development the future Rothschilds may become sacks of shining sovereigns."

Mr. R. L. Dugdale has written a book entitled, "The Jukes," in which he shows that in seven generations a single abandoned home bequeathed to the world twelve hundred descendants, a large majority of whom were idiots, imbeciles, drunkards, lunatics, paupers, prostitutes, and criminals. Seven hundred and nine of the twelve hundred have been registered, and their history studied in this terrible book. He finds that harlotry in the community at large averages not quite two out of every hundred women; it was over twenty-nine times more frequent among the "Juke" women. In the line of Ada Juke, better known as "Margaret, the Mother of Criminals," it was found that crime among the men was thirty times greater than that in the community in general. Of the five hundred and thirty-five children born, nearly twenty-four per cent were illegitimate. Among the women of this Juke family the number of paupers was seven and a half, and among the men nine, times greater than in the community at large. Summing up the crimes and pauperism of this single family, Mr. Dugdale estimates that in seventy-five years it cost the public over one million two hundred and fifty thousand dollars, without reckoning the cash paid for whisky, or taking into account the entailment of pauperism and crime of the survivors in succeeding generations, and the incurable disease, idiocy, and insanity growing out of this debauchery, and reaching farther than we can calculate.

But, you say, what have all these terrible and startling facts to do with the licensed liquor saloon? I answer, Much! every way.

It is the legitimate effect of the goods that are sold in the liquor saloon to excite and inflame every lust and passion that degrades and brutalizes humanity. The saloon and the brothel are often combined into one; and they go hand in hand, with the closest possible fellowship. They are the gigantic twin corrupters of the youth of America. You cannot hurt one of them without hurting the other. Not long ago the *Wine and Spirit Gazette* made this frank confession: "The Phillips' law, passed by the legislature of Ohio, forbidding the sale of liquor in the houses of ill-fame, went into effect on May 25. The importers of champagne in this city are beginning to feel the loss of business in Ohio. Piper Heidsieck representatives in Cincinnati claim that the enforcement of the law in the big cities of Ohio will cost them forty thousand dollars annually; Munn company representatives estimate their loss at thirty thousand dollars; importers of Pomerey Sec claim that they will lose sixty thousand dollars; and the other importers will suffer proportionate losses. The local brewers, also, feel the effects of the law, as many of the houses in Cincinnati and Cleveland sold large quantities of beer." How clearly this reveals the sensitive nerves of kinship between the liquor saloon and the house of prostitution!

The social influence of the saloon alone is enough to condemn it forever. There are, no doubt, exceptions; but no man can successfully deny that, as a class, the saloon-keepers in this country are of the lowest character. "They are impure, profane, irreligious, vulgar, and often criminal; and their saloons are like themselves. In no place as here — outside of the brothel —

is the atmosphere so saturated with all that is vicious and corrupting. Here one meets with the world's filthiest characters, filthiest pictures, and filthiest conversation; because here congregate society's filthiest souls." The saloon is the stem around which cluster all the festering vices of the community. A leading worker for reform in New York says that the suppression of the curse of strong drink would include the destruction of ninety-nine out of every one hundred of the houses of ill-fame; that each of these brothels is an unlicensed liquor saloon, whose parlor is in every sense a bar-room, where strong drink is freely dispensed. By suppressing this drink business — this prime source of crime — we would stop the supply of raw material for these criminal houses, and make it impossible to keep the victims already thus employed. A missionary on going at the written request of one of these lost women to rescue her from a den of infamy, remonstrated with her for being even then slightly under the influence of drink. "Why," was her indignant reply, as tears filled her eyes, "do you suppose we girls are so dead that we have lost our memories of mother, home, and everything good? No, sir; and if it were not for liquor and opium, we would all have to run away from our present life, or go mad by pleadings of our own hearts and home memories. I don't know one girl," she continued, referring to her numerous associates, "that does not either drink or use morphine!"

A recent report of the chaplain of the Magdalen Society of New York shows that of eighty-nine fallen women in the asylum at one time, all but two ascribed their fall to the effect of the drink habit. A lady missionary makes the statement that of two thousand sinful women known personally to her, there were only ten cases in which intoxicating liquors were not largely responsible for their fall. George Frederick Parsons, in his famous *Atlantic Monthly* articles, made a striking comparison between the practices of modern society in legalizing the liquor traffic and the horrible cruelty of ancient times. "The ancient Greeks," says Mr. Parsons, "had inherited the practice of infanticide from savage ancestors. They became so inured to it that when the custom of exposing children gradually superseded child-murder, there were not wanting moralists to deplore the change as denoting the rise of what moderns would call a 'sickly sentimentalism.' The fate of exposed children, sad though it was, elicited no practical sympathy. When a Greek mother thus abandoned her infant, it was what her neighbors did. It was social crime disguised by custom. If we are prepared to be candid with ourselves, it may not be difficult to show that even the barbarism of ancient Greece is not so far behind us as we should like to be able to feel that it is. We do not kill our children. We do not any more expose them after the antique mode. We cherish them in their infancy, rear them to adolescence, and then send them forth to put their immature vitality against the most elaborate, skilfully devised, and comprehensive machinery for mincing human beings that the world has ever seen."

A physician of Boston was standing on a street corner in New York City on the day of General Grant's funeral, waiting for a street-car. Another gentleman, a stranger to him, stood by his side. Suddenly a loud voice shouted from behind, "Can you show me the way to hell?" They both turned, when a drunken man staggered toward them, repeating his question, "Can you show me the way to hell?" The other gentleman seemed nonplussed; but the physician stepped to one side, and pointing to the white lettering on the glass which his back had concealed, said: "Here it is. This is the guide-board — 'Beer Saloon.' You are not out of the way. This is a sure road; many have gone this road before you, and you will find plenty of companions."

It is against the liquor saloon, as the most aggressive, the most lustful and dangerous, foe of the purity of social life that I call you to give your immediate and continued antagonism. This is a question where there can be no doubt as to where lies the right and the wrong. Abraham Lincoln said about slavery, "If slavery is not wrong, then nothing is wrong." So I say to you, "If the saloon traffic, with its train of disease and lust, is not wrong, then nothing is wrong." The saloon is the moral lazar-house of society. All the rivers of the earth could not wash it clean, and all the winds of heaven cannot carry off its foul stench. To license such an incarnation of diabolism for gold, much or little, is the darkest blot on the civilization of our times.

In the name of the pure mother who bore you; in the name of the innocent children who climb on your knee, and nestle in your arms, and call you father or mother, brother or sister, or friend; in the name of all goodness as opposed to all badness in modern society, — I call upon you to put your influence, your prayer, your speech, your vote, in deathless antagonism to the saloon!

ITEM NUMBER THREE.

THE SALOON DEBTOR TO RUINED HOMES.

THE American home that is true to its heritage in this Republic "of the people, and by the people, and for the people," is the proudest fortress of modern civilization. Men who have always lived in the midst of thickly populated regions, where home-life generally prevails, do not know how to appreciate the home-life at its full worth. Born and reared as I was in the far West, living up to my early manhood in the midst of frontier conditions, seeing much of life in mining-camps where great multitudes of men were gathered together without the restraining and comforting influences of home, I know by contrast the divine power of a good home. The home is the conservator of everything that is good. No matter what trickery or fraud or selfishness a man may have to contend with in the day's business, or how bitter and cynical it may make him, if he comes back to a clean, pure, loving home at night, in the presence of a true, fond wife, and the caresses of innocent children, all his bitterness and selfishness vanish away. Home-life, with the generous, unselfish love of kindred, is a sunshine which awakens into growth all the truest impulses of a man's being. It is impossible for any man to go from his home to his business in the morning with the kiss of a good woman upon his lips, and the soft caress of baby fingers lingering in pleasant memories on his neck, without feeling more of brotherliness for his fellows, a truer confidence in human nature, and a deeper devotion to make himself worthy of such holy affection. Communism and anarchy have their sternest foes and their surest antidote in the clean, pure homes of the people. It is not often that a man goes out from a noble home, no matter how humble it may be, where his spirit has been elevated by the blessed influences of womanhood's homage, and childhood's clinging tenderness has lingered about him — rare indeed it is that a man goes from a scene like that to excite riot, or to conspire against the safety of the community.

Anything that attacks the home as an institution, that invades its sanctity, that degrades father or mother or children, that takes from it not only the physical comforts but the mutual confidence and love which make it a place where weary men grow strong again, and worn and nervous women are refreshed and encouraged; anything that renders it an unsafe place for children to grow up into a pure and healthy manhood and womanhood, loving God and hoping the best for humanity; anything that stands in antagonism to the safety, the purity, and the peace of the home — is the most deadly enemy to the church, the state, and civilization.

One of the sternest indictments that can be made against the saloon is that it is the most deadly foe of the American home that was ever conceived. If Satan himself were to call a convention of all the haters of humanity, of all the cold-blooded and cruel spirits on earth or in hell, nobody would believe that the combined counsel of their evil intelligence would ever be able to devise anything more effective in its power to destroy home-life than the licensed liquor saloon. The liquor saloon has the capacity of absorbing everything that is beautiful and pure and joyous in the home; itself, meanwhile, becoming no better. It is the mongoose of our civilization. Many of you doubtless have read in Rudyard Kipling's jungle stories the vivid description of Rikki Kikki's fight with the snake. The hero of the story is the mongoose. The mongoose was introduced into Jamaica some twenty years ago by the sugar planters, who hoped in that way to kill off the rats which preyed upon their crops of sugar-cane. The mongoose is a marvelously prolific animal, having three breeding seasons a year, and producing from five to thirteeen little mongooses at every birth. As a rat-killer, the mongoose is a great success; and it was not very long before a rat was a rare article in Jamaica. But as the supply of rats failed, the supply of mongooses increased, and this industrious little animal began to enlarge his bill of fare. First he took in black crabs, ground-birds, snakes, toads, and insect-destroying birds. As these disappeared, very naturally beetles, flies, moths, and ticks multiplied. And still the mongoose filled the land, until now he destroys young pigs, kids, lambs, calves, puppies, kittens, all kinds of poultry, all kinds of game such as quail, guinea fowl, snipe, and ground-doves, and all sorts of birds that nest near the ground. He is not satisfied even with animal life; for dessert he has learned to enjoy bananas, pine-apples, young corn, pears, sweet potatoes, cocoa, and peas. Fish, also, he devours; and, indeed, as necessity comes on, he seems capable of eating up everything that is of precious value to humanity on the whole island of Jamaica.

Now, the liquor saloon is the mongoose of this country. Dr. Rainsford says that it is the poor man's club, and that as such it must be protected and defended; that, indeed, he needs it so badly that it must be kept open on Sunday, so that he may have a chance to spend his hours of leisure there; that the laboring-man, so tired and worn out with his day's work, must have some pleasant place where he can get away from his narrow tenement-house rooms, and while away his resting hours. It is strange that these dear brethren like Dr. Rainsford forget that these narrow tenement-house rooms are good enough for the wife and the babies seven days in the week, and seven nights as well. But the trouble is, the saloon, which its defenders say must be perpetuated as the poor man's club, to eat up the rats of his leisure hours, and furnish him a place to kill time, isn't satisfied with that kind of fare. This licensed mongoose not only gulps down the workingman's leisure, but it swallows without blinking his hard-earned money, his physical health and strength, his good temper, his love for his wife, his fondness for his children; and then, seeking for new worlds to conquer, it goes on eating up the necessary food for his family; it eats up the shoes off the little girl's feet, the coat off the little boy's back, and the roses out of their mother's cheeks, and all that was sweet and pure and holy in their once happy home.

A commercial traveler who had been accustomed to drink quite freely with his comrades, astonished them by saying, when the bottle was passed in the smoking-car one day, "No; I won't drink with you to-day, boys. The fact is, boys, I have sworn off." He was greeted with shouts of laughter by the jolly crowd around him. They put the bottle under his nose, and indulged in many jokes at his expense; but he refused to drink, and was rather serious about it.

"What's the matter with you, old boy?" sang out one. "If you've quit drinking, something's up; tell us what it is."

"Well, boys, I will, though I know you will laugh at me; but I'll tell you all the same. I have been a drinking-man all my life, and have kept it up since I was married, as you all know. I love whisky; it's as sweet in my mouth as sugar, and God only knows how I'll quit it. For seven years not a day has passed over my head that I didn't have at least one drink. But I am done. Yesterday I was in Chicago. Down on South Clark Street a customer of mine keeps a pawn-shop in connection with his other business. I called on him; and while I was there a young man of not more than twenty-five, wearing threadbare clothes, and looking as hard as if he had not seen a sober day for a month, came in with a little package in his hand. Tremblingly he unwrapped it, and handed the articles to the pawnbroker, saying, 'Give me ten cents.'

And, boys, what do you suppose it was? A pair of baby's shoes; little things, with the buttons only a trifle soiled, as if they had been worn once or twice. 'Where did you get these?' asked the pawnbroker. 'Got 'em at home,' replied the man, who had an intelligent face and the manner of a gentleman, despite his sad condition. 'My wife bought 'em for our baby. Give me ten cents for 'em; I want a drink.' 'You had better take those back to your wife. The baby will need them,' said the pawnbroker.

"'No, she won't; because she's dead. She's lying at home now; died last night.' As he said this, the poor fellow broke down, bowed his head on the show-case, and cried like a child.

"Boys," said the drummer, "you can laugh if you please, but I — I have a baby of my own at home, and by the help of God I'll never drink another drop."

Then he got up and went into another car. His companions glanced at each other through dim eyes and silence. It did not seem to be funny to anybody. No one laughed; but somehow the bottle disappeared ; and soon each was sitting in a seat by himself, pretending to read a newspaper.

Don't for a moment imagine that this is a strange, unique, and exceptional case. It is the legitimate business of the licensed liquor saloon to do that kind of work in the home-life of the people. It is a wreckage business from first to last. If a wrecker builds a false light on the coast, and lures a vessel to destruction, so that he may plunder the bodies of the drowned sailors, he is sent to the penitentiary or the gallows. But if he is a cunning enough wrecker to come and build his false light on the street-side in Brooklyn, he can have a special dispensation granted for his benefit by the city government and under State law; and every policeman's button and club that he sees passing up and down the street will be pledged to defend him in carrying on his devilish business.

A good home where love abides, and where each member of the family not only feels sympathy and tenderness for the others, but where there is a mutual pride in each other's goodness and strength; where the children look up to father and mother with loving admiration, always thinking of them with chivalrous fidelity; and where father and mother think of their children with pride in their innocency, and fond ambition for their success and triumph in life, — such a home is the mightiest fortress for the courage of the individual members of the family that could be devised or imagined. One goes out from a home like that with the assurance of a general when his base of supplies is impregnable and abundant. But how many times the liquor saloon makes its insidious entrance into such a home, and strikes the dagger to the very heart of all that peace and comfort! Many a home I have known that had in it everything heart could wish until such an enemy invaded it, and afterward all its seeming grandeur and beauty was but a hollow mockery. Gold was yet left in abundance, the mansion was still there, the carpets were as soft, the table as heavily loaded, the books and pictures as abundant and beautiful as ever; but the peace, the confidence, the heart, had gone out from that once blessed abode.

Mrs. Mary A. Livermore has recently retold the story of a battle in the South-west under General Thomas. The Federal troops had gained a great victory; and General Thomas, on a high vantage-ground, watching the fleeing hosts, and hearing the shouts that rent the air, exclaimed, "It was Geary's men that won the fight! How splendidly they behaved! How magnificently he handled them! Where is he? Bring him here, and we will wait for him! He must be congratulated, promoted, brevetted on the spot!"

The staff-officers ran in one direction and another to find him; for it was thought by some that he was leading the pursuit, and by others that he had gone to his tent.

At last he was found in his tent, sitting in the dim light of a candle fastened in the upturned handle of a bayonet, his arms folded, his figure bent, every feature of his face indicating despondency. His brother officer rushed in and took him by the hand, "Geary, I congratulate you! It is your men that have won the day! How magnificently they behaved! It is to you we are indebted for the victory; and

I am sent by General Thomas to escort you to the field, where he and his staff-officers wait, and you are to be brevetted on the field. I thank God that you did not receive a scratch! I thought you were gone three or four times, as I saw you in the thick of the rain of iron hail."

"Oh, do not congratulate me! do not congratulate me; I cannot bear it! Tell General Thomas I cannot come. Excuse me to him. Tell him I do not care for promotion. Tell him I do not ask anything in the way of congratulation."

"Why, you don't expect I will go back to General Thomas with an answer like that. Rouse yourself, man! It is the inevitable result of reaction after a battle. Let me take you to General Thomas. You are not wounded; nothing has happened to you. You are all right. You haven't a scratch."

"Oh, I am wounded!" said General Geary; "I am wounded; I am so sorely wounded that never again shall I know any surcease of pain! I am so sorely hurt that there is no surgery in all the world that can heal my wound! I am mortally wounded; I am shot through the heart!"

"Why, what do you mean?" asked his friend. "Your appearance, except your depressed spirits, does not indicate the least injury!"

Then, rising, General Geary walked over to the corner of the tent, and turned back a blanket, revealing the dead body of his only son, his chief of staff, who, galloping beside his father in the hot pursuit, had received a minié ball through the heart. The father, seeing him reel in the saddle, took him upon his own horse, and rode back to his tent, the sounds of rejoicing seeming to him like mockery, and the victory like defeat.

So you and I know men and women who are mortally wounded, who have been shot through the heart. The young life that was dearer to them than their own has received a death-wound more terrible than a rifle-ball ever gave; for that can only destroy the physical life, while the good name, the pure manhood, the noble soul, are left unsullied. I know men who have seen the liquor saloon take not only the physical life of their sons, but take also their good name, defile their pure minds, debauch them and degrade them, until they were but pitiful human wrecks. Who knows how to measure a sorrow like that? And yet every year there are multitudes of homes in Brooklyn that are being thus marred and blighted; and it is the natural, logical work of the licensed liquor saloon to do just that.

I would to God I could arouse every one here to-night to a generous fight in behalf of those who are being wounded and oppressed and destroyed by the liquor saloon. Let us not think only of our own homes, but let us so live and so act that the homes of the poorest and humblest shall be safe. God has so ordered the universe that one insures best his own care, and the good of those that are specially dear to him, by giving himself to generous, self-denying service to all.

Possibly some of you have heard Major Hilton tell an incident which once occurred while he was on the Scottish coast. Just at the break of day the people of a little hamlet on the coast were awakened by the boom of a cannon over the stormy waves. They knew what it meant, for frequently they had heard before the same signal of distress. Some poor souls were out beyond the breakers, perishing on a wrecked vessel, and in their last extremity calling wildly for human help. The people hastened from their houses to the shore. Out there in the distance was a dismantled vessel, pounding itself to pieces. Perishing fellow-beings were clinging to the rigging, and every now and then some one of them was swept off into the sea by the furious waves. The life-saving crew was soon gathered.

"Man the life-boat!" cried the men.

"Where is Hardy?"

But the foreman of the crew was not there, and the danger was imminent. Aid must be immediate, or all would be lost. The next in command sprang into the frail boat, followed by the rest, all taking their lives in their hands in the hope of saving others. Oh, how those on the shore watched their brave loved ones as they dashed on, now over, now almost under the waves! They reached the wreck. Like angels of deliverance they filled their craft with almost dying men — men lost but for them. Back again they toiled, pulling for the shore, bearing their precious freight.

The first man to help them land was Hardy, whose words rang above the roar of the breakers, "Are you all here? Did you save them all?"

With saddened faces the reply came: "All but one. He couldn't help himself at all. We had all we could carry. We couldn't save the last one."

"Man the life-boat again!" shouted Hardy. "I will go. What! leave one there to die alone? A fellow-creature there, and we on shore? Man the life-boat now! we'll save him yet."

But who is this aged woman with worn garments and disheveled hair, with agonized entreaty falling upon her knees beside this brave, strong man? It was his mother!

"O my son! your father was drowned in a storm like this. Your brother Will left me eight years ago, and I have never seen his face since the day he sailed. No doubt he, too, has found a watery grave. And now you will be lost, and I am old and poor. Oh, stay with me!"

"Mother," cried the man, "where one is in peril, there's my place. If I am lost, God will surely care for you."

The plea of earnest faith prevailed. With a "God bless you, my boy!" she released him, and speeded him on his way.

Once more they watched and prayed and waited — those on the shore — while every muscle was strained toward the fast-sinking ship by those in the life-saving boat. At last it reached the vessel. The clinging figure was lifted and helped to its place, where strong hands took it in charge. Back came the boat. How eagerly they looked and called in encouragement, and cheered as it came nearer!

"Did you get him?" was the cry from the shore.

Lifting his hands to his mouth to trumpet the words on in advance of their landing, Hardy called back above the roar of the storm: "Tell mother it is brother Will!"

ITEM NUMBER FOUR.

THE SALOON DEBTOR TO PAUPERIZED LABOR.

The claim is sometimes made that the liquor traffic employs a great many men, and that if it were done away with the world would be full of idlers, thrown out of employment because of the discontinuing of a large industry. But it is very easy to show that this is only one of the devil's sophistries. It is not hard to get at it in so simple a way that any of these boys and girls here can understand. The liquor business is represented by hundreds of millions of dollars, and employed in a certain year, not long since, five hundred and thirty-one thousand, one hundred and sixty-eight men. According to the United States census statistics, it requires $3,505.75 invested in liquor manufacturing, to employ one man. In the ten leading industries of the United States, representing that same year a capital of nearly $3,000,000,000, it required only $1,021 to give employment to a single man. Now, you can easily see that if you take the money used in manufacturing death and destruction in our domestic, social, and national life, and turn it into legitimate channels, it would give employment to more than three times as many laborers as it now does. Oh, but, somebody says, that would lead to over-production. But, my friend, I assure you that it is not over-production that is the matter with us in the legitimate channels of trade. It is under-consumption, because the money is wasted in dissipation and vice.

Suppose you look at it from another standpoint. Eighteen per cent of the product of the ten leading industries of the United States is paid to labor as wages, while only 10 per cent of the product of liquor manufacture goes to labor. Thus the liquor business helps indirectly to foster a monopolistic class. Put the money invested in liquor manufacturing into legitimate trade, and nearly twice as much of the income goes to labor.

Look at it from still another standpoint. The value of the liquor product, compared with the capital invested, was on a given year 1.22

per cent, while the value of the product of the ten leading industries, compared with the investment, was 1.93 per cent; so it is easy to see that if you invest the liquor money in other business the result will be a proportionate increase, in the wealth produced, of 71 per cent, of which nearly twice as much goes to labor as now. And it is a safe thing to say that whatever benefits labor is of the greatest possible benefit to business at large; for, after all, the laborer is the great consumer of the world.

If the $900,000,000 annually spent for liquor, and the great majority of it by laboring-men, was to go next year for boots, shoes, clothing, food, books, magazines, pictures, and education, there would be such a revival of business throughout the world that we should think the millennium had arrived. The bugbear of overproduction would be dispelled at once. More goods of all kinds would be demanded, more would be manufactured, multiplied labor would be required to make and sell them, wages would advance, and every class of society would feel a tremendous uplift.

I have been led, during the past few years, to give a large amount of attention to the sorrowful life led by the very poor in our cities. I have looked with pity upon the starved and hopless victims of the sweat-shop. In pursuit of these studies I have shivered in winter and melted in summer in the dens and attics of slum tenement houses. As I have come to know something of the heart-breaking miseries which really exist in our great cities, I have grown to hate as a monster more intolerable to me than ever before this Moloch traffic in strong drink, which gorges itself, year after year, with ten times enough of the good gifts of God's providence and man's industry and genius to feed every hungry stomach, clothe every ragged back, and comfortably house every homeless family in the land. It is worse even than that. It not only gorges itself on these wholesome gifts of God, but it digests them into a witch's broth that tempts to moral disaster and ruin multitudes of the harassed and wretched beings who have already been plundered by its cruel rapacity.

The distinguished Roman Catholic Bishop Ireland, in an earnest address to the Irish people of America on the injurious results of the saloon, says: "Compute in any one city the sums of money spent by Irishmen in Irish saloons, and you will be affrighted. In one Western city of America there are fifteen hundred saloons kept by Irishmen for the benefit of Irishmen. Allow the average receipts of each saloon to be fifteen dollars a day, and you have an annual expenditure for liquor by the Irish of that city of $8,212,500. Add to these sums the value of time lost by drink, of wages unearned because men visit saloons, and $12,000,000 per annum is not too high a figure to represent the annual losses to the Irish of one city. Repeat the calculation with due proportion from St. Paul to New York, from Boston to Philadelphia, and you will know," says this earnest bishop, "why we are poor. It is idle talk to advise the people to secure homes of their own, to leave the crowded cities, to gain by labor and economy a competence for themselves and their families; we must lay the ax to the root of the evil, first teaching them to shun the saloon, which is swallowing up their earnings."

The bishop's closing figure of swallowing reminds me of the story of Tom, who met an old friend, who was formerly a prosperous young lumberman up in Northern Minnesota, but whose bad habit of drinking brought him to a pretty "hard up" condition.

"How are you?" asked Tom.

"Pretty well, thank you; but I have just seen a doctor, to have him examine my throat."

"What's the matter?"

"Well, the doctor couldn't give me any encouragement. At least, he couldn't find what I want to find."

"What did you expect him to find?"

"I asked him to look down my throat for the saw-mill and farm that had gone down there in drink."

"And did he see anything of it?"

"No; but he advised me if ever I got another mill to run it by water."

Dr. Theodore Cuyler, who addressed us with such eloquence and earnestness last night, aptly calls the saloons "Banks for Losings."

He said the only interest paid on deposits is in redness of eyes, foulness of breath, remorse of conscience, and loss of health, happiness, and character. Every one who makes a deposit gains a loss. One man goes into the bank with a full pocket, and comes out empty. Another goes in with a good character, and comes out with the word "drunk" written upon his bloated countenance. Many a clerk with a good situation has entered one of these "Banks for Losings," and when he came out his situation was gone. Many prosperous business-men have lost their business in these banks. I knew an old neighbor, who lived the next farm to us when I was a boy, who lost a farm a mile square and a big herd of cattle, a stableful of fine horses, a flock of sheep, and several thousands of money on interest. He deposited them all in the saloon in a country town five miles away; and I saw him after the last cent was gone, and his wife had died of a broken heart, and his children were wandering waifs, a poor, old, ragged, staggering bankrupt. If a correct sign were posted over the door of the Brooklyn saloons to-night, there would be a great deal of astonishment as the people went down through the streets to-morrow to business. They would read, if we were to follow Dr. Cuyler's figure, something like this: "Banks for Losings. Open at all hours. Nothing taken on deposit but good money. Nothing paid back but disgrace and disease, degradation and death. An extra dividend of delirium tremens will be paid to old depositors. A free pass to hell insured to those who pay well at the counter. Tickets to all cemeteries, entitling the bearer to a drunkard's grave in the pauper section. All children of depositors sent without charge to the orphan asylum or the almshouse — for other people to support." I submit to you that that would be an honest sign of the regular, every-day business which is expected of the licensed liquor saloons of the city of Brooklyn.

How ridiculous it is for the political demagogues and party bosses to tell us that we must continue the liquor saloons in order to make business lively, or to keep down the taxes and support the government! It reminds me of a juggler out at Lewiston, Idaho, and his experience in fooling a company of ignorant Indians. The juggler went around among the Indian wigwams, and did not attract very much attention until he seemed to take a fancy to a small dog, with which he finally made friends by patting and petting him. He asked the Indians how much they would take for him; to which they replied that they did not want to sell him. The juggler said, "Him very valuable dog," at the same time rubbing him down the back to his tail, at each stroke taking a handful of money from the end of his tail, also from his mouth, ears, and nose. At these strange proceedings the Indians stood in awed astonishment, and naturally were more determined than ever not to part with so valuable an animal; and as soon as the juggler left, they took the dog down to the river-bank, and killed and dissected him; but to their great chagrin and sorrow, they found that the wily juggler had taken all the money out of him. And I can tell you that the saloon-keeper gets all the money there is out of the liquor dog. There is none in it for the people who have to pay the taxes, and care for its disease and crime.

There is none in it for the poor man who wastes there his wages. The only man who makes money out of the liquor traffic is the man who makes the liquor and sells it. And in the long run, the greatest loser of all is the great army of laboring-men who are ruined and debauched by it.

Mr. Joseph Medill, for many years one of the most distinguished journalists of the West, testified before a Congressional committee of labor and education to what I am sure would be backed up by men of careful and intelligent observation everywhere. He says: "I have rarely known a steady, sober, industrious man, who saved his surplus earnings and prudently invested them, but attained independence before old age; and I have never known a workman, no matter what might be his wages, who freely indulged his appetite for liquor, that ever made any headway. And," continues Mr. Medill, "the money thus thrown away on liquor by the wage-workers in the last ten years would have provided each family with a home free of rent, thereby emancipating all of them from servitude to landlords. If invested in railroad stocks and bonds during the last ten years, it would have transferred the ownership of every single mile of railway in the United States to the labor classes who squander their wages on drink. Drink is the evil progenitor of the worst ills which the poor man encounters, and is the chief cause of the bad luck which keeps him in poverty. The wage-classes cannot support in idleness a quarter of a million of saloon-keepers and their bartenders and families, and pay the rents of their dram-shops, and hope to prosper themselves."

Strange it is that men will be so blind as to rob themselves and their own families of the comforts of life, to support another family in idleness and luxury! We are told of a drinking man who related to his family one morning a strange dream he had had the previous night. In it he saw three cats — a fat one, a lean one, and a blind one; and he was anxious to know what it all meant. His little boy answered quickly, "I can tell what it means. The fat cat is the saloon-keeper who sells you the drink, the lean cat is mother and me, and the blind cat is yourself."

A little boy in Covington, Ky., who was the child of a man who had recently stopped drinking and signed the pledge, said one morning,—

"Father, are you always going to wear that blue ribbon?"

"I hope so, my dear," was the reply.

"So do I," said the little one.

"Why do you hope so?" asked the father.

"Because I have never had so many strawberries in my life as I have had since you signed the pledge and put on that blue ribbon."

A laboring-man cannot expect to buy strawberries for two families. If he supports the saloon-keeper, you may depend upon it his own family will go hungry.

In one of our large cities a laboring-man, leaving a large saloon, saw a costly carriage and pair standing in front, occupied by two ladies elegantly attired, conversing with the proprietor.

"Whose establishment is that?" he said to the saloon-keeper as the carriage rolled away.

"It is mine," replied the dealer proudly. "It cost thirty-five hundred dollars. My wife and daughter cannot do without it."

The mechanic bowed his head a moment in deep thought; then, looking up, said with the energy of a man suddenly aroused by some startling flash, "I see it! I see it!"

"See what?" queried the saloon-keeper.

"See where, for years, my wages have gone. I helped pay for that carriage, for those horses and gold-mounted harnesses, and for the silks and laces for your family. The money that I have earned, that should have given my wife and children a home of our own, and good clothing, I have spent at your bar. My wages, and the wages of others like me, have gone to support you and your family in luxury. Hereafter my wife and children shall have the benefit of my wages; and, by the help of God, I will never spend another dime for drink."

No amount of legislation, and no power that can be obtained by trade unions or labor combinations, can be of any real help to the laborer who spends his money in the liquor saloon. Dr. J. O. Peck, of blessed memory in this church, used to tell of a man he knew who crossed Chelsea Ferry to Boston one morning, and turned into Commercial Street for his usual glass. As he poured out the poison, the saloon-keeper's wife came in, and confidently asked for five hundred dollars to purchase an elegant shawl she had seen at the store of Jordan, Marsh & Co. He drew from his breast pocket a well-filled pocket-book, and counted out the money. The man outside the counter pushed aside his glass untouched, and laying down ten cents, departed in silence. That very morning his devoted Christian wife had asked him for ten dollars to buy a cloak, so that she might look presentable at church. He had crossly told her he had not the money. As he left the saloon he thought, "Here I am helping to pay for five-hundred-dollar cashmeres for that man's wife, but my wife asks in vain for a ten-dollar cloak. I can't stand this. I have spent my last dime for drink." When the next pay-day came, that meek, loving wife was surprised with a beautiful cloak from her reformed husband. She could scarcely believe her own eyes and ears as he laid it on the table, saying, "There, Emma, is a present for you. I have been a fool long enough. Forgive me for the past, and I will never touch liquor again." She threw her arms around his neck, and the hot tears told her heart-felt joy, as she sobbed out, "Charley, I thank you a thousand times. I never expected so nice a cloak. This seems like other days. You are so good, and I am so happy." And when the great, strong fellow told Dr. Peck about it, he couldn't keep back the tears, and declared it was the happiest day he had seen in ten years.

But I cannot stop without again calling your attention to the folly, the lack of business sense, and the wickedness of the city or state licensing in the midst of workingmen these "Banks for Losings." And every one of us who, by our influence or our vote, or by our neglect or indifference, helps to establish or maintain the liquor saloon in the community, is thus contributing to the institution which, more than all other institutions combined, robs and debauches the laborers of the land.

ITEM NUMBER FIVE.

THE SALOON DEBTOR TO LAWLESSNESS AND CRIME.

THE licensed liquor saloon breeds lawlessness and crime by necessity, from the very conditions of its existence. It is the natural nest for the outlaws who resist the civilization of the latter days of the nineteenth century. If you have never been in the slum districts of Boston or Chicago or New York City, and I were to come to you and describe the horrible depravity of the vicious elements that control those sections, were to tell you of the vice and crime, the debauchery and lewdness, that reign there, and then were to propose to draw a diagram of the streets that run through those awful sections, and describe the business that was carried on there by saying to you that on the first corner was a Baptist Church, and that from there on down to the next corner the street was blocked solidly with dry-goods houses, and at the foot of that street there was a Methodist Church located, and across on the other side of the street there were other stores of good character, and in the middle of the block a Presbyterian Church, and were to go on describing the whole section of the city as filled with schools, reputable business houses, and churches, it would be impossible for you to believe my statement that the debauchery and crime which I had before indicated could exist in relation to these other things. And if I were to ask you what kind of business you would expect to be carried on in such a slum district, you would answer without a moment's hesitation, if you were honest, "Liquor saloons and their children — gambling-hells and brothels;" and that is exactly what you will find in every slum district of every city in the world.

Some of you remember very well when what is known as Five Points in New York City was perhaps the nearest like perdition of any place on the American continent. And when the newspapers of the city turned the attention of the public to the outrageous outlawry which existed there, they found that the center of

Five Points and all its diabolism was an old brewery, and that every street running out from it was lined with liquor saloons. And when the Christian element of the city undertook to elevate Five Points, and clean it up, the very first thing they did was to buy the old brewery, and change it into a city mission.

A number of years ago I happened to be up in the Calapooya Mountains in Southern Oregon. I was staying at the house of an old farmer, who, desiring to show me the courtesies of the region, asked me if I would like to see some deer-hunting. And it did not take me long to say yes. He called his eldest boy, Abner, and sent him, with three or four hounds, across the pastures, into the great forest a mile and a half away; while we, each taking a gun, went in almost the opposite direction. After we had climbed a long hill through the timber, we came to a slight opening; and the old man said, "Whenever the hounds start up a deer over in that forest where Abner went, he always makes a circuit around over that hill yonder, crosses the creek away to the right, and coming up through this opening, runs between that great spruce-tree and that old snag there that has been struck by lightning." We waited; and soon we heard the deep baying of the hounds, — at first faint in the distance, but rapidly drawing nearer, — and before we had been lying in ambush twenty minutes, a great buck with wide-spreading antlers leaped out of the brush, and stood directly between that old snag and the big spruce-tree, and lost his life in the determination to follow through the woods the beaten trail to which he was accustomed. Now, then, criminals have their runways the same as other animals. And if a man were to commit a brutal crime in Brooklyn or New York to-night, and then leave for Chicago, the police would get a description of the man, and telegraph the chief of police there to arrest him. When he gets to know the kind of man he has to deal with, — that he is a vicious man, capable of the most brutal crimes, an old jail-bird, and a natural associate of criminals, — what sort of places in the city of Chicago would the chief of police have watched in hope of finding his game? Do you think he would order a close watch on all the prayer-meetings?

Would he send his best detectives to the art galleries and the public libraries? No, indeed; you know very well they would go to the saloons and the institutions that are born of the saloons — the brothels and gambling-hells; because that kind of game always seeks such runways for their familiar ground.

The fact is, that the liquor saloon is at heart an outlaw. The only effective way to deal with it is to take it for what it is, a criminal, and deal with it as a criminal. When you can tame a gambling-hell, and make it a safe resort for young men; when the Ethiopian can change his skin, and the leopard his spots, — then you may hope to draw the teeth of a liquor saloon. Nothing but the hard fist of the Ten Commandments, with the police power of the city and State and nation behind it, can deal with such an institution. The Chicago *Inter-Ocean* says: "The saloon element is not amenable to ethical eloquence, or the logic of reason; the remedy lies in taking the offender by the scruff of the neck and the slack of the trowsers, metaphorically speaking, and throwing him into court."

Other countries as well as our own are coming to understand the serious danger from the spread of alcoholism. *La Petit Journal* of Paris, a newspaper which has the largest circulation of any paper in the world, made the assertion in a double-leaded editorial, that "of all the dangers menacing our agricultural population at the present day, the gravest and most difficult to fight is alcoholism." The *Tageblatt*, of Leipsic, also says: "It will not be possible to produce any law adapted to really put a stop to the evil of drunkenness without relinquishing some of our popular national conceptions about interference with individual liberty." The German saloon-keepers of this country, that have had so much to say about prohibitory laws interfering with personal liberty, ought to listen to this cry from home.

One of the most dangerous features of our modern civilization is that the saloon strikes at the very existence of law and order in our large cities. Here is an actual occurrence in the city of Chicago within less than two years. A saloon-keeper in that city plied with intoxicants a young girl of previous good character, and then brutally outraged her. He was arrested under the grossly inadequate statute which punishes the sale of intoxicants to minors. I would not be afraid to offer a hundred dollars to any one in this large audience who could in a hundred trials guess the quibble upon which the police justice, who was the tool of the liquor saloons, released this criminal scoundrel, for whom hanging would have been too good. This was his august decision : "There is only one minor in this case," said this judicial scoundrel, "while the law says minors." According to his interpretation of the law, the criminal must drug two young girls at one time before he could be held to be guilty of an offense against the law. And yet so great was the power of the liquor traffic in the city of Chicago, that, although the matter was publicly commented upon by the press, he continued to disgrace the court of justice, as Paddy Divver continues to do in New York City to-day.

Come down to Cincinnati. One Monday morning a woman stood in the police court, and by her side stood two stalwart policemen. The charge which the clerk read against her was disorderly conduct on the street and disturbing the peace.

"Who are the witnesses against this woman?" asked the judge; and the two policemen stepped forward to be sworn.

"Now tell the story," said the judge, and one of them began:—

"I arrested the woman in front of a saloon on Broadway on Saturday night. She had raised a great disturbance, was fighting and brawling with men in the saloon, and the saloon-keeper put her out. She used the foulest language, and with an awful threat struck at the keeper with all her force. I then arrested her, and took her to the detention house, and locked her up."

"The next witness will take the stand," said the judge. And then the second policeman stepped up and corroborated his fellow.

"Call the saloon-keeper."

"What do you know of the case?"

"I know dis vomans vas making disturbance by my saloon. She comes and she makes troubles, und she fights mit me, und I put her de door oud. I know her all along. She vas pad vomans."

Turning to the trembling woman, the judge said, —

"This is a pretty clear case, madam; have you anything to say in your defense?"

"Yes, judge," she answered in a strangely calm though trembling voice. "I am not guilty of the charge, and these men standing before you have perjured their souls to prevent me from telling the truth. It was they, not I, who violated the law. I was in the saloon last Saturday night, and I'll tell you how it happened. My husband did not come home from work that evening, and I feared he had gone to a saloon. I knew he must have drawn his week's wages, and we needed it all so badly. I put the little ones to bed, and then waited all alone through the weary hours until after the city clocks struck twelve. Then, I thought, the saloons will be closed, and he will be put out on the street. Probably he will not be able to get home, and the police will arrest him and lock him up. I must go and find him, and bring him home. I wrapped a shawl around me and started out, leaving the little ones asleep in bed; and, Judge, I have not seen them since."

Here the tears came to her eyes, and she almost broke down; but, restraining herself, she went on,—

"I went to the saloon where I thought most likely he would be. It was about twenty minutes after twelve; but the saloon, that man's saloon"—pointing to the saloon-keeper, who now seemed to want to crouch out of sight—"was still open, and my husband and these two policemen"—pointing to those who had so lately sworn against her—"were standing at the bar, drinking together. I stepped up to my husband, and asked him to go home with me; but the men laughed at him, and the saloon-keeper ordered me out. I said, 'No; I want my husband to go with me.' Then I tried to tell him how badly we needed the money he was spending; and then the saloon-keeper cursed me, and told me to leave. Then, I confess, I could stand no more, and I said, 'You ought to be prosecuted for violating the midnight closing law.' At this the saloon-keeper and policemen rushed upon me, and put me into the street; and one of the policemen, grasping my arm like a vice, hissed in my ear, 'I'll get you a thirty days' sentence in the workhouse, and then we'll see what you think about suing people.' He called a patrol wagon, pushed me in, and drove to the jail; and, Judge, you know the rest. All day yesterday I was locked up, my children at home alone, with no fire, no food, no mother."

Her story was so manifestly true, that that judge did have the honor to dismiss this woman; but the liquor traffic had such power in the city of Cincinnati, that this perjured scoundrel of a saloon-keeper and these lawless policemen were never prosecuted, and the policemen were not even laid off for a day. This case is a matter of record in the Cincinnati court.

But why enumerate the cases? There is not a city in this land which the liquor traffic does not disgrace by its lawlessness and crime.

The liquor traffic is the only business under heaven bad enough to be accused of corrupting such a police force as the recent investigation shows has been governing the city of New York. From the days of the whisky rebellion in South Carolina, down to the shameless defiance of the excise laws of the city of Brooklyn, it has been and is a lawless institution. There is scarcely a green mountain in all the South that has not been reddened with the blood of United States officers who have been slain by its emissaries. So lawless is the liquor traffic, that when, after the hanging of the anarchists in Chicago, the press reports carried the news over the country that a number of Sunday-schools had been established in that city in which the principles of anarchy and hatred of American institutions were taught, nobody was astonished, or questioned the additional statement that every one of these schools of anarchy was held either in a liquor saloon or a room leading out of a bar-room.

It is the commonplace of the census reports and the every-day statistics of crime to tell you that more than three-fourths of all the crime which curses the land is born and bred in the liquor saloon.

Strange it is, indeed, how silent Christian men and women can be on a subject of such mammoth importance! I have heard the story of the father of a family, who was accustomed to ask a blessing on the family meal when there was only his own household present; but when there was company at the table he did not have the courage to do it, and omitted the invocation. One day when he did this, his little daughter stopped him in carving with the inquiry, "Say, papa, ain't you going to make that funny little noise in your throat?" It is the shame of our time that there are so many Christian people, so many men of ability and power and influence, who see all the iniquity of the saloon, who behold its ravages, who are burdened with taxes to support its disease and crime, and yet dare not make even "a funny little noise in their throats" in the presence of this infernal traffic.

ITEM NUMBER SIX.

THE SALOON DEBTOR TO POLITICAL CORRUPTION.

In a country governed like ours, every question, first or last, which is of serious interest to human life, comes to be a political question. You cannot confine the saloon question to the region of moral suasion, whether in the home, the Sunday-school, or the church. We have been seeing from night to night, in this series of conferences which we have had, that every species of vice, degradation, and crime grows out of the saloon. It is impossible to make all these crimes the subject of political consideration and punishment, and leave the very mother of crimes outside the realm of politics.

The saloon has invaded politics on its own account. It stuffs the ballot-box, elects its tools to office by bribery, buys legislatures, and in every way tarnishes the fair name of American political life. We base the right of the political destruction of the liquor traffic on the bed-rock truth that the government has a right to defend its own life. To use an illustration once used by John B. Finch: Suppose a man comes here with a club to kill me. Under the laws of this country I would be compelled to retire as far as I could with safety; but when the issue is between his life and my life, he must die; because every man has the right to defend himself. I am a man; and, so long as I obey the law, I have a right to be a man. I exist; and, until I forfeit that right by my own actions, I have a right to exist. This is the foundation of social and political ethics.

A story is told of a muscular preacher who was a sort of Peter Cartwright species of divine, and used all the powers the Lord had given him — fists as well as tongue. Some of the good sisters in his church thought he was too much inclined to use his fists, so they sent him this text: "If a man smite thee on thy right cheek, turn to him the other also." They thought they would puzzle the old man to harmonize the text and his conduct. He said he would preach from it the next Sabbath, and he did. He opened with the usual services, took his text, and went ahead. He went on to say that the Bible was distinguished from all other books by appealing to the God-man, and not to the brute-man. He continued, "If a man should strike you on the right cheek, he might do it through mistake, or might do it through a feeling of mischief; and if you turned around without asking any questions and struck him back, that would be acting like a brute. You should keep still, and turn the other cheek. If he strikes you on that, you know that he meant it; then go for him."

That may not be a very good Bible interpretation; but I agree with Finch that it is a good interpretation of the law of this country, the law that is inherent in every individual — the right of self-defense. The government has a right to defend its own life. If war were to break out to-morrow, and the emergency should demand it, it would have a right to draft me from this pulpit, the lawyer from his clients, the physician from his practice, and every business-man here away from his business, put its uniform on our backs, and guns on our shoulders, and send us out to fight for the life of the country. The government has a right to destroy any business that threatens the life of the country, or that debauches the character of its citizens. The Supreme Court of the United States has decided this again and again; and finally, with reference to the liquor traffic, in these very words: "The government has the right, through its police power, to protect its own life."

This whole question, then, is rightfully a political question. Now, I know I am not telling you anything new when I say that the saloon thrusts its filthy hand into politics on every possible occasion. The saloon never touches politics except to defile and corrupt. Just at this time we are having an immense amount of discussion from the pulpit, in mass meetings, in legislatures, and, above all, in the great newspapers and magazines, about municipal reform. But I thoroughly agree with a Western editor who says that there cannot be any permanent municipal reform in this country so long as America tolerates the saloon. Men who know how political campaigns in municipal affairs are managed will not accept a nomination many times, because they know that by common custom it makes them the helpless prey of every beer-slinger in the city. It has often befallen candidates for high judicial honors — men without a stain upon their names or a vice of which they could be accused, and men, even, who were running on so-called reform tickets — that they have been led about from bar to bar like a fat ox, that they might win the vote of the slums by free beer. Nothing so speaks to us the degradation of politics as this. In most of our cities the Sabbaths before a municipal election are simply pandemonium let loose. The bartender poses as the dictator of American destiny. There is no candidate of a political party too lordly to do him obeisance. Between the great rival parties he consciously holds the balance of power. His royal scepter is a beer faucet. A barkeeper in Richmond, Va., hearing some talk of a reform movement in municipal politics, laughed it to scorn with these words: "Any bar-room in Richmond is a bigger man in politics than all the churches in Richmond put together." Shut up the saloons, and municipal politics would reform themselves. Chauncey M. Depew is frank enough and brave enough to say that he has no doubt that Tammany Hall will very soon be in control of New York City again, and will probably continue to govern it during the present generation. And yet such an unspeakably rotten machine would have absolutely no chance to govern New York City if it were not for the corruption of politics through the liquor traffic. So long as the saloon door stands ajar at every corner of the street, the affairs of cities will probably be managed by the men who are not above purchasing the privilege from the breweries.

Before the recent upheaval in New York City, the New York *Herald*, in an editorial protesting against the rum-besotted misrule of that city, said: "We must no longer be ruled by graduates of the Tombs and nurslings of the grog-shop." But how useless it is to cry out against harvesting the crop we have deliberately planted and nourished. A city will and must be governed by the graduates of its own institutions. If it establishes and maintains two hundred grog-shops to one high school, it cannot complain that more graduates from the former than the latter come into mastery.

The trouble in our politics has been in the past, and is to-day, that the saloon has laid its corrupting hand upon every party that has shown indications of probable supremacy in the near future.

Dr. Cuyler well said the other evening, and Dr. Dixon repeated the same sentiment last night, that there is absolutely nothing under present conditions to expect from either of the leading political parties in the way of opposition legislation to the liquor traffic. As Dr. Cuyler said, we have had a Democratic legislature in Albany, and obtained no reform legislation against the liquor traffic from it ; and now that we have a Republican legislature, we not only do not expect anything from it as against the saloon, but are compelled to work tooth and nail to keep them from repealing the Sunday law, and doing for us a great deal worse than their Democratic predecessors. One who has studied the history of the two parties in various sections of the country for the last few years, says that you will find it hard to decide which should bear the palm for truckling subserviency to the liquor traffic. Looking at the two, one is irresistibly reminded of the dialogue between two young students of the Westminster Catechism.

"Joe, how fur have you got?"

"I'm right in the middle of original sin," answers Joe.

"Oh, I'm furder'n that!" says Jack; "I'm beyond redemption."

Now, I do not intend to discuss party politics to-night in any offensive way, or to urge upon your attention any political party; but it is certainly within the province of the present discussion to emphasize what you must all admit to be a fact — that the liquor traffic, with its licensed saloon system, holds such a grip upon each one of the three leading political parties (if it shall be true that the Populist party shall continue to have a leading influence) as to utterly palsy them in both hand and lip on the line of anything that means really serious hurt to the saloon. They talk pleasant platitudes now and again in resolutions and platforms; but they never say to us — and the filthy hand of the liquor traffic holds them so tightly by the scruff of the neck that they cannot say to us — that if we will help them into power they will put the hoof of that power on the head of the liquor traffic. If you go through the South, you will find that in all those States the great body of temperance men, the men who believe in righteousness in law and conduct, are in the Democratic party. No man who has ever lived in the South, or traveled there with a carefully observant eye, will deny this fact. The public-spirited citizens, the men of wealth, of education, of moral character, the men who hate the saloon, and would like to see it dead, are, in an overwhelming majority, members of the Democratic party. Take, for instance, the whole Methodist Episcopal Church South — fully as strong there in proportion to the population as is the Methodist Episcopal Church in the North — the church that believes in the prohibition of the liquor traffic as thoroughly as we do; and that entire prohibition church, with its enormous membership, from the bishops to the last layman who has come in, is in the Democratic party. But while this is the fact, there is also a large contingent of the Democratic party in the South that is interested in the manufacture and sale of intoxicating liquors, and the saloon holds its grip on the party to such an extent that it is always able to thwart prohibition and turn its legislation into license. If we come into the Northern States, where most of you are better acquainted, and contrast these two parties with reference to the liquor traffic (and I am not comparing them in any other relation to-night), we find here just the reverse of what we do in the South. The Republican party is undoubtedly, as compared with the Democratic party, the temperance party. That is, it has in its membership an overwhelming majority of the public-spirited citizens of the community who are opposed to the liquor traffic, who hate it and abhor it, and would rejoice exceedingly to see it stamped out of existence. And yet, in the North as in the South, we get license instead of prohibition in most cases, when it comes to legislation; and the leading newspapers of national reputation in the party have declared unequivocally that prohibition must be prohibited within the Republican party. The same trouble exists here as in the South — that while the great majority of temperance men are in the Republican party here, as they are in the Democratic party there, there is a large contingent in the Republican party throughout the Northern States that is interested in the manufacture and sale of intoxicating drinks. And so again the dirty hand of the liquor saloon grips party conventions and legislatures by the throat, and turns legislation into license instead of prohibition.

It reminds me of a dime museum advertisement which I used to see on the fences over in Massachusetts, which declared that there was in one of the museums of Boston a two-headed man. The advertisement, which probably lied, said that the man had two well-formed heads and two necks, but that the necks ran down into one stomach, so that he had only one pair of arms, and one pair of legs. When he ate and drank, talked and sang, or when he prayed or cursed, he was two men; but when it came to digesting his food, or to going about, he was only one man. He could be two men while he was sitting still talking; but when he got up to go and accomplish anything, there was only one pair of legs that carried off the whole menagerie.

Now I say, with all due respect to the great political parties — and every man should treat great combinations of his fellow-men with respect — that the condition of the Democratic party in the South, and the condition of the Republican party in the North, seem to me to be aptly illustrated by that figure. Taking the Republican party in this State at the present time as a sample — only because it is nearest to us; for the Democratic party in Georgia would serve the purpose just as well — is it not true that it has two definitely formed, distinctive heads so far as its attitude to the liquor traffic is concerned? One of those heads is a temperance head. It is a beautiful head. Perhaps you remember a picture that two or three years ago was in the *Review of Reviews*. It was called the composite photograph of Gladstone's cabinet. In some way the photographer manages to so arrange a number of photographs that he gets the distinctive features out of all the faces, and the result is a composite, or average photograph of all of them. Well, now, this temperance head of the Republican party is a composite photograph of all the nice and good men there are in it — bishops (Protestant and Catholic, Methodist and Protestant Episcopalian), doctors in divinity, editors, college presidents, elders and deacons, class-leaders and stewards. Many of my dearest friends, the people for whom I have the greatest respect and regard, help to make up the composite photograph of this beautiful temperance head in the Republican party. At the same time there is another head. And no matter how devoted a man may be to his party, he must admit this. There is a plainly defined whisky head to the Republican party. It is a horrible-looking head. To make up this composite picture you must let brewers and distillers, retail saloon-keepers, bloated drunkards, race-track gamblers, prize-fighters, bullies, and thugs of every conceivable stage and grade of brutality and viciousness, sit for their picture; and the result is the whisky head of the Republican party. The two heads run down through their necks into one stomach, whose greatest interest is party supremacy. During the greater part of the year the two heads talk and act very differently. The temperance head preaches sermons, sings hymns and psalms, prays prayers, utters temperance resolutions, talks prohibition and eternal opposition to the saloon. All this time the whisky head edits liquor organs, curses the temperance fanatics, drinks unlimited quantities of beer and bourbon, and swears eternal allegiance to the traffic. But the curious fact about it all is, that there is only one digestive apparatus and one pair of legs to this queer monstrosity; and whenever it starts up to do anything in the city council, or in the legislature, the two big license legs carry off both heads into the saloon camp. One may pray and protest, the other may curse and shout victory, but both of them go. And the result reminds me of a little doggerel epitaph, which it is said may still be descried on the tombstone that marks the resting-place of a deceased maiden over on the New England coast, —

> "She had two bad legs and a badish cough,
> But 'twas her bad legs that carried her off."

It is the bad license legs of these political parties that carry them off every time.

What is needed above everything else is that the men who love their country more than they do the spoils of office shall come out of all these parties, and arraying themselves together upon some broad platform for righteousness, smite the liquor saloon to its death. I do not say it shall be the Prohibition party. All the intelligent prohibitionists that I know anything about are willing to meet their brother haters of the saloon on any common ground, under any name, so that it means death to the liquor traffic.

Why cannot this be done? The legalized traffic in intoxicating liquors is the bitterest curse physically, intellectually, socially, politically, or morally, that has ever smitten with shame the fair face of the Republic! Compared with the crime, poverty, and suffering caused by the drink traffic, the silver question and the tariff question lumped together are a contemptible bagatelle. And yet, despite the universally admitted magnitude of this giant evil, there appears to be a wicked conspiracy of silence on this subject among the leaders of the great political parties. East and West, North and South, earnest, God-fearing men, year after year, beg at party conventions for some adequate recognition of the evil, and some honest threat of hostility to the liquor traffic. And they are treated with insolence and contempt, while the saloon-keeper is flattered and fawned upon with disgusting humility.

The deadly lethargy which hangs over Christian circles calls for outspoken leadership on the part of all Christian ministers if the sluggish hosts of righteousness are to be roused to action.

Modern civilization has no more pitiable sight than is revealed when brewer and Catholic priest, distiller and Protestant clergyman, saloon-keeper and Sunday-school superintendent, bartender and class-leader, stand shoulder to shoulder, voting twin ballots, and obsequiously supporting the party policy which sustains this conspiracy of silence concerning the hideous cancer which is eating out the very heart of our institutions. We cannot shut our eyes nor close our ears to the unspeakable sorrows of our brothers and sisters around us. Ravished homes, staggering drunkards, broken-hearted wives, pitiful orphans, meet us every day, and appeal to us on every street.

We Christians are set in the midst of this misery, as disciples of the Nazarene, to do what we can to steady these staggering feet, heal these broken hearts, and awaken to hope these despairing souls. But at every effort we make we are confronted in fiendish antagonism by the liquor traffic, which the State itself protects, and from which it receives money — money with as damnable a smirch upon it as any that ever Judas handled. For every church in Brooklyn, Catholic or Protestant, there are multiplied saloons backed by the city and State and national governments, and protected by the police.

What is there left to us, Christian brothers, when confronted with facts like these, but to make our protest so loud, so dangerous, and so effective, that it cannot pass unheeded? I feel compelled to say that I am profoundly convinced that just so long as Christian ministers and laymen continue to pray, and pass resolutions, and preach sermons, and sign petitions, like prohibitionists, but continue to vote like saloon-keepers, just so long will they be treated with the practical contempt they deserve by all political parties.

HOW TO SETTLE THE SALOON ACCOUNT.

IN our six previous conferences we have discussed the several items in the account which society holds against the liquor traffic. We have found that the saloon as an institution is a prolific cause of disease, and an enemy to the health of the people. We have found also that it excites and inflames the brutal lusts and passions, and honeycombs the community with social and private immorality. We have taken note of the fact that it is the most deadly enemy of the home; that no home is so sacred or pure, or hedged about with such protective influence, as to be sure that it may not be invaded by this ruthless foe. We have seen that the laboring-man has no enemy so tyrannical or so pitiless as the liquor traffic; that no legislation nor any change of sociological conditions can be of any permanent benefit to the laboring-classes of the world so long as $900,000,000 a year are wasted in intoxicating drinks. We have found that the saloon is the hotbed of lawlessness and crime; that it is the natural school of anarchy; that out from its doors go directly the influences which cause the ruin of three-fourths and more of all those who in jails and penitentiaries and reformatories are suffering for their misdeeds. We have gone into the realm of political life, and have seen there the same corrupting and disastrous influence — that the saloon is the caucus hall for everything that is vile and dishonest and shameful in our politics. Thus we have gone around the circle of physical, intellectual, social, domestic, economic, and political life, and everywhere we have found that the saloon is a heavy debtor to humanity. It blesses nowhere; it curses everywhere.

We have drawn these six indictments against the saloon; and, alas! how many more might have been drawn. The New York *Tribune* said some time ago, in an editorial article on the liquor traffic: —

"It is impossible to examine any subject connected with the progress, the civilization, the physical well-being, the religious condition of the masses, without encountering this monstrous evil. It lies at the center of all political and social mischief. It paralyzes energies in every direction. It neutralizes educational agencies. It silences the voice of religion. It baffles penal reform. It obstructs political reform. There is needed something of that sacred fire which kindled into inextinguishable heat the zeal of the abolitionists and compelled the abandonment of human slavery, to rouse the national indignation and abhorrence against this very much greater evil."

No license system has ever had any permanent or practical effect in diminishing the woes of the saloon. License has been tried in almost every form that could be imagined, high and low, for more than a hundred years, and it has never lessened either drunkenness or the amount of liquor sold. We have just seen a great fight in this city, led by good Christian men and women, to secure the refusal of a license for a saloon near the entrance to the Brooklyn Bridge. I am glad they succeeded, and congratulate them on their courage and their triumph. And yet I cannot but feel, and they cannot but feel, that, after all, it was an empty victory. If there were no other saloons in all that region, then it would be a victory worth winning; but all about there, on almost every corner, are other gaping liquor hells, that go on day and night, week-day and Sunday. Anybody that wants liquor down there has it just the same, and it may be doubted whether there is any less liquor sold because one saloon more or less is planted in the midst of such a group of dens of iniquity.

We have been passing, during the last few years, through a fad of high license, compared with that which is low. And I am sure that the most that can be said about it anywhere is what the polite and considerate serving-man said to his master, who, in hunting, had fired into a flock of game and hit none of them, "Well, sir, you've made 'em shift their places." High license may make whisky barrels "shift their places," but it has never diminished them.

The master's failing to hit his game reminds me of a story they tell over in New England; how up in the old post-office at North Andover a group of men were sitting around the stove one morning, gossiping about neighborhood affairs, when a new-comer suddenly burst open the door, and exclaimed, —

"Say! heard the news? Old Deacon Pettingill's barn is all burned up."

"You do tell! you do tell!"

"Yes; and not only his barn, but all his hay, and his wagons and his cattle — the whole thing is burned up."

"My! My!" says one. "Why, it will break poor old Deacon Pettingill all up. Say, 'Zekiel, you haven't told us how it happened."

"Well, you see there was a man coming down the road with a gun on his shoulder, a shotgun, and he got along opposite old Deacon Pettingill's barn, and he saw a big owl a-sitting right on the peak of the barn, and, like a fool, he just up and fired away, and the waddin' caught fire in the hay, and jist burned up the whole affair."

Again there were exclamations of execration on the folly of the man with the gun, and a great deal of sympathy expressed for old Deacon Pettingill in his great loss. There was one old fellow, however, a typical old Yankee, who would make a good picture of Uncle Sam, who hadn't been saying anything, but during the excitement had been occasionally practising at squirting the tobacco juice through his teeth at a certain little broken corner of the stove door. As the excitement began to subside, he sent a good shot through the stove-door, and, looking up at the new-comer with a knowing wink, said composedly, "I say, 'Zekiel, did he hit the owl?"

All our talk and our license systems amount to nothing unless they hit the owl of the liquor traffic. And the truth is that no license system that has ever been invented has done that. The statute books of all civilized nations are lumbered up with license laws, and have been for many years, and yet the drunkards reel through the streets of all their cities, and the victims of the saloon lie in all our hospitals. This train of disease and misery springs out of the license system itself, and it will never die out until the system is abolished. If the whole brood of drunkard-makers were to be drowned in the Atlantic Ocean to-morrow, and the whole army of suffering victims were to find rest in the grave, the sharks would not have time to pick the bones of the one, or the grass to carpet the graves of the other, before another brood of drunkard-makers would spring up, and another army of tipplers gather about their dens, unless you should destroy the accursed license system which produced them.

But high license, you cry. What difference does the size of the license make in the case? Do you suppose the brandy that makes a man's heart beat thirteen times a minute faster than it ought under low license, will only make it beat five times too often under high license? Do you suppose the bourbon whisky that, under a license fee of a hundred dollars, eats holes in a man's throat and stomach, and makes him from lips to stomach one raw, burning sore, will become mild and healing if the tax be raised to a thousand dollars? Will the beer that clogs a man's liver and rots his kidneys when drunk over a pine table in a saloon that pays fifty dollars a quarter suddenly become healthful when poured from a silver pitcher over a marble table in a saloon which pays three hundred dollars a quarter? Will the drunken brute beat his wife and kick his children the more gently when made drunk under high license than he would under low license? Out on all such nonsense! The stronger and the more elaborate your license system may be, the more thoroughly it intrenches the saloon as a disease and crime scattering center in the community.

The utter folly of supposing that any kind of license system can stay the ravages of the liquor traffic, or heal the wounds it makes upon society, is clearly seen whenever you apply it to an individual case, and think how horrible it would seem to you if a man were to offer you so many dollars for the opportunity to ruin your boy under any other circumstances. One can easily imagine a dialogue like this:—

The father and mother are sitting together by the fireside at night. The mother says, "Our boy is getting to be out late at night."

The father replies, "Well, we must tax the saloon fifty dollars."

A little later there is another scene, and the mother says, "Husband, I believe John drinks."

And the father replies, "We must put up that tax to one hundred dollars."

A year passes by, and they are sitting together again. The mother's face looks very sad and anxious; and we hear her saying, "My dear husband, our boy is being ruined."

"Well," says the father, "we must try the license a while at two hundred dollars."

Only a few months pass now, when the heart-broken mother meets the father at the door, and exclaims, "Oh, my God! my boy came home drunk."

"Well, well! we must make it three hundred dollars."

Time passes again. The father has been away on a journey, and comes home. The poor, faded mother meets him, and says, "Just think, William, our boy is in jail!"

The father begins to get mad now, and cries out in impatience, "I'll fix those saloons! Tax 'em four hundred dollars!"

Still later they meet, and the mother wails, "My poor child is a confirmed drunkard!"

And the father replies, "Up with that tax! Make it five hundred dollars!"

Still later I hear the mother saying, "Our once noble boy is a wreck."

And the father says, "Now I will stop them; make it six hundred dollars."

It is only a little later. There is black and white crape on the door. The hearse stands in front, and up-stairs the poor, broken-hearted mother cries, "Alas! alas! we carry our poor boy to a drunkard's grave to-day."

"Ah," says the father, "I was too lenient. We must regulate this traffic; we ought to have made that tax one thousand dollars."

You say that dialogue is absurd. Is it more so than our method of dealing with this murder-making saloon? This whole thought of license is not only absurd, but it is abominably wicked. Even the queen of Madagascar rebuked the United States by replying to those who proposed that she should receive a revenue from strong drink: "I cannot consent as your queen to take revenue from that which destroys the souls and bodies of my subjects." License fees are the price of blood. If Judas had received three hundred pieces of silver instead of thirty for the betrayal of Christ, it would not have made the 'transaction any the less infamous.

Nothing but absolute prohibition touches the people's hurt from the liquor traffic. To use another illustration from that inimitable prohibition orator, John B. Finch: Suppose you should go home to-night, and when you get there, you find your boy on the bed. He has been indisposed for several days, and you see that he is sick. You put your hand on his head — it is burning hot; you put your finger on his pulse, and find it running above a hundred. You speak to him. He answers in broken sentences. You at once send for a physician. When he comes, you ask, —

"What is the matter with Willie?"

The physician makes an examination of the boy's body, asks how he has been feeling for the past few days, and tells you that Willie has the fever. He says, "The child has taken, through the nose and lungs, malarial poison. The fever and the increase of pulse are simply nature's effort to expel the poison and save the child's life. This increased activity of the vital forces is simply nature defending herself against the poison which would destroy the organism unless expelled."

You ask, "What shall we do for Willie?"

The medical man answers, "I will leave medicine to help nature to do its work, and will tell you how to nurse him."

Then you ask, "Doctor, how long before he will get well?"

And his reply probably will be, "When the poison has been entirely overcome and cast out."

Now, the fact is that the saloon is a poison center in our body politic. There arises from it a deadly malaria which permeates every department of our life, and unless it is cast out it must finally cause destruction.

Abraham Lincoln said in his day, "The nation cannot exist half slave and half free." So I say in mine, The Republic cannot live half drunk and half sober. The only hope of permanent progress and stability to our institutions is in casting out this deadly poison that is destroying the life of our people. Cast it out, not by trying to regulate the stream of misery, as one might regulate the flow of water by a faucet; but stop the cause of it. That is the path of wisdom.

The folly of the license system reminds me of Bridget, who had been told by her mistress to scrub the kitchen floor. Opening the door a while afterwards, she found Bridget with the water two or three inches deep, and mopping for dear life, while the water still flowed from the faucet.

"Why don't you turn off the faucet, Bridget?" exclaimed the lady.

"Sure, ma'am, it's mesilf that hasn't toime, the water kapes me a-moppin' so fast."

They tell me that in some insane asylums they utilize this same idea to find out whether patients that have been improving are sufficiently sane to be allowed to go home. They take them to a close room with a bare floor, turn on the faucet, and give them a mop, and tell them to mop it dry. If they have sense enough to be allowed to go home, they turn off the faucet at once. If not, they mop away until taken away to their ward again. Whenever the time comes that we are really sane, we will turn off the faucet of this infernal traffic.

HOW TO SETTLE SALOON ACCOUNT. 125

How silly it is for us to go mopping away with missions and orphan asylums and Keeley cures — and be content with that — when we have it within our power to turn off the whole tide of drunkenness, disease, and crime by abolishing the traffic itself!

Oh, but, you say, you must not violate personal liberty. How incongruous seems this cry of personal liberty from the lips of the saloon-keeper! As another has well said, if liberty has fallen so low that her defenders are the class of men who debauch the manhood, the womanhood, and the civilization of this country, God pity liberty! The idea of these men arrogating to themselves the position of special champions of the liberties of this people is absurd, ridiculous, and nonsensical. It makes me think of an illiterate church-member by the name of Walker, in Southern Illinois. During a revival where his spiritual strength had been renewed, the idea came into his mind that he ought to preach. He called upon the officers of the church, and told them that he believed God had given him a special call. They expressed some doubts, promised to consider his case, and sent him away. A few days later he returned, still more fully impressed that it was his divine mission to defend the religion of the Lord Jesus Christ, and to turn sinners from the path of death. The officers of the church asked him if he had received any new evidences of his call. He responded, "I went home from this yer meetin', troubled an' perplexed, an' the nex' day I went ter visit neighbor Jones on the hill. Comin' back late in the evenin' 'cross the paster, the thought come to me that ef God had reely called me he oughter make it manifest to me thar. So I jest knelt down in a clump of bushes, raised up my voice in prayer, and asked God to show me my dooty. Jest as I was a-prayin', on the stillness broke an awful voice, sayin', 'Go, Wa-alk-er, W-a-lker, Walker! Go, Pr-e-e-a-cher, Pr-e-a-cher, Pr-e-a-ch-e-r-r-r!'" The officers of the church examined the source of the call, and found that it was a jackass, which, alarmed at his praying, had commenced to bray. For the life of me I cannot shake off the idea that this call of the liquor dealers as the defenders of liberty must have come from some such source.

But what is their cry? They say, "Personal liberty;" they mean, sensual or natural liberty. There is a vast difference between civil liberty, to insure which the noblest spirits of the race have been willing to give life itself, and this personal liberty for which the liquor seller asks. Unrestrained natural liberty is the enemy of civil liberty. It was personal liberty that enabled the assassin Guiteau to shoot down President Garfield; it was civil liberty that made him swing from the gallows for that act. It is personal liberty that permits the saloon-keeper to sell intoxicants that set on fire the vicious lusts and wicked passions of his victims, and stimulate every form of iniquity and crime; it will be civil liberty, after we have national prohibition, that will pour his poison into the gutter, and send him, if he persists in his abominable business, to the penitentiary.

One of the most distinguished medical men in London relates that one of his friends, a gentleman who is a great scholar and antiquarian, has spent many thousands of pounds in collecting the history of London, and pictures relating thereto, including exhibitions of Bartholomew Fair, Tyburn, the Savoy, and those horrible old prisons of the cruel, earlier days. One night when he was looking through that collection, he was horrified by one picture. Though accustomed to see death in all forms, he turned pale at that picture. It related to a debtor's prison. There was a punishment which debtors only a little over a hundred years ago sometimes underwent. They were put into a cell in which a dead body was allowed to lie; and when it could be retained there no longer, another was put in its place! You exclaim in horror, "Could such a thing be only a little more than a hundred years ago?" It could and did; and if one hundred years hence some man shall stand as we stand now, and refer back to the current Brooklyn daily press accounts of the disease and misery and crime licensed by the liquor saloon, his audience will be overcome with incredulity and horror.

Christian brothers, let us take up this struggle with renewed courage! Let us compel political parties to fight the saloon or count us out! Let those taunt us who will about "voting in the air." It is better a thousand times to "vote in the air" than to deposit your ballot in a beer barrel, and help maintain the rule of rum. Let us go on "voting in the air" until the atmosphere is charged with the electricity that presages the thunderbolt of doom to this infamous traffic.

Broderick the Brave, standing undaunted before an exultant and despotic slave power, said: "Slavery is old and decrepit and dying; but freedom is young and strong and vigorous." So the licensed liquor traffic is old and rotten with its own corruption. It is a jailbird of innumerable crimes, whose bloated face is familiar in every rogues' gallery on the face of the earth. Strong and arrogant as it seems, it is really staggering to its execution.

Prohibition is young. The dew of young manhood is on its brow. The sunshine of a new chivalry streams upon its path. The strength of righteousness flows in its veins. The courage of immortal hope is in its heart. There is but one issue to such a struggle. The saloon shall die!

...LIFE OF...
GEN. CLINTON B. FISK

PREPARED BY

PROF. A. A. HOPKINS.

The life of a man of national repute. His remarkable career from boyhood, through his business and military life, to his nomination for Prohibition President of the United States. The biography has been brought down to the time of death and burial of the General. 12mo, cloth, about 300 pages. Illustrated with excellent portrait. Price, $1.00, postage free.

This Biography, prepared (with the General's approval) by Prof. Hopkins, who enjoyed free access to all the General's private papers, is very accurate and complete. It is of permanent and standard value to the American people. It is purely American in its examples, patriotic in all its teachings, and will inculcate in the rising generation the deepest self-respect, and excite to greater energies the noblest ambitions. It is the record of a self-made man; the biography of a typical American life; a charming story, reaching from the log cabin of a pioneer to positions of national honor.

Our expectations of great things in the detail and progress of his life are never disappointed. Nor is it surprising to learn of his intimacy with such men as Lincoln, Greeley, and Grant; his distinguished service in the Civil War, wherein he won his well-earned commissions; his endearment to both the whites and blacks of the South, and his popularity among the mixed multitude of the North, East, and West; his splendid business career, and noble Christian activities; his championship in many patriotic movements; his eminent social qualities, eloquent oratorical abilities, philanthropic spirit, and his well-known temperance principles.

FUNK & WAGNALLS COMPANY,
30 Lafayette Place, New York.

Prohibition:

THE PRINCIPLE,
THE POLICY, AND
THE PARTY.

A Dispassionate Study of the Arguments For and Against Prohibitory Law, and of the Reasons Governing the Political Action of Its Advocates. By E. J. WHEELER. Third Edition. 12mo, cloth, 227 pp., 75 cents. Postage free.

CONTENTS.

PART I.—THE PRINCIPLE.

1. The Legal Phase of the Subject. 2. Two Views of the Province of Government. 3. John Stuart Mill and Herbert Spencer. 4. The Question of Personal Liberty. 5. The Sin Per Se. 6. The Controversy over Bible Wines. 7. Physiological Effects of Alcohol. 8. Drink and Crime. 9. Drink and Death. 10. The Economical Evils of Drink. 11. Political Evils Due to the Saloon. 12. The Pleasure of Drink. 13. Recapitulation.

PART II.—THE POLICY.

1. The Inquiry Instituted by the Canadian Parliament. 2. The Result in Maine. 3. The Result in Vermont. 4. The Result in Kansas. 5. The Result in Iowa. 7. The Attitude of the Liquor Dealers. 8. Legal and Moral Results of Prohibition. 9. The Demand for National Prohibition.

PART III.—THE PARTY.

1. Can the Reform be Accomplished Through Either Old Party? 2. The Balance of Power Plan. 3. The Non-partisan Plan of Union. 4. The Objections to a New Party. 5. Is Public Sentiment Ready? 6. Other Issues of the Day.

APPENDIX. (OVER.)

STRONG LANGUAGE FROM
STRONG THINKERS.

CHAIRMAN DICKIE says: "Mr. Wheeler's book contains the very bed-rock argument for our reform."

BISHOP FITZGERALD writes: "It is the best presentation of the subject I have seen."

GEN. CLINTON B. FISK: "It is by far the best thing yet published on Prohibition."

JOHN LLOYD THOMAS writes: "It is a most masterly treatment of the fundamentals of our reform."

JUDGE BRIGGS: "It is a great book. It is the most coherently logical book from beginning to end that I have ever read."

H. C. BASCOM says: "Condensed, impartial, searching, convincing, and scholarly, are adjectives that can do the book but meagre justice."

THE VOICE says: "All the questions involved are stated with perfect fairness and answered with ability — *with unsurpassed ability* we are disposed to say."

BISHOP JOHN H. HURST writes: "I am delighted with it. It covers the whole ground. I regard it as the most valuable contribution of the day to the growing literature on the subject."

MISS WILLARD says: "In my judgment we have not since the beginning of the controversy had a keener Damascus blade than this little volume. I believe the person who can read it and remain in the old parties is a *lusus naturæ*."

FUNK & WAGNALLS COMPANY,
30 Lafayette Place, New York.

(SEE OTHER SIDE.)

www.ingramcontent.com/pod-product-compliance
Lightning Source LLC
Chambersburg PA
CBHW020110170426
43199CB00009B/469